Heaven's
Not a
Crying Place

Joey O'Connor is a best-selling author of five books for parents and young adults. He lives with his wife and three children in Southern California.

His works include:

Breaking Your Comfort Zones: And 49 Other Extremely Radical Ways to Live for God
Excuse Me! . . . I'll Take My Piece of the Planet Now
Whadd'ya Gonna Do? 25 Secrets for Getting a Life
Where Is God When . . . 1001 Answers to Questions Students Are Asking
You're Grounded for Life: And 49 Other Crazy Things Parents Say

For speaking events, conferences, and seminars, please call (714) 369-6767. You can also write to Joey O'Connor at P.O. Box 3373, San Clemente, CA 92674-3373.

Heaven's Not a Crying Place

Teaching Your Child about Funerals, Death, and the Life Beyond

Joey O'Connor

Fleming H. Revell
A Division of Baker Book House Co
Grand Rapids, Michigan 49516

© 1997 by Joey O'Connor

Published by Fleming H. Revell
a division of Baker Book House Company
P.O. Box 6287, Grand Rapids, MI 49516-6287

Second printing, December 1997

Printed in the United States of America

Library of Congress Cataloging-in-Publication Data

O'Connor, Joey, 1964–
     Heaven's not a crying place / Joey O'Connor.
         p.   cm.
     ISBN 0-8007-5643-6 (pbk.)
         1. Children and death—Religious aspects—Christianity.
     2. Bereavement—Religious aspects—Christianity. 3. Consolation.
     I. Title.
     BV4906.026   1997
     248.8′66—dc21   97-37895

Unless otherwise noted, Scripture is from the HOLY BIBLE, NEW INTERNATIONAL VERSION®. NIV®. Copyright © 1973, 1978, 1984 by International Bible Society. Used by permission of Zondervan Publishing House. All rights reserved.

Scripture identified GOD'S WORD is from GOD'S WORD and used by permission. Copyright 1995 by God's Word to the Nations Bible Society. All rights reserved.

"Sibling Grief: How Parents Can Help the Child Whose Brother or Sister Has Died" by Marcia G. Scherago is reprinted with permission.

"When You Wish upon a Star" is used with permission of The Compassionate Friends.

For current information about all new releases available from Baker Book House, visit our web site:
                                http://www.bakerbooks.com

For more information about Joey O'Connor's books and Internet links for parents, teenagers, and kids, visit Joey's web site: http://www.joeyo.com. You can e-mail Joey with your comments and questions at: joey@joeyo.com

For the Ricciardi family—Chuck, Loretta,
Matthew Charles, and Faith Marie

Contents

Acknowledgments

Most writers write about topics they enjoy writing about. My previous books are filled with humor and funny stories that I hope will be useful to the parents and young people who read them. I wish I could say that this is one of those books, but death is just not a very funny subject . . . unless, of course, you grew up in a family with six siblings and a one-hundred-year history of the family funeral business. (Yes, we even had a dog called "Lily" who was named after Herman Munster's wife on the hit '60s TV show *The Munsters*. That's probably the subject matter for another book.)

I like to make people laugh, but this book made me cry. *Many times.* This was a difficult book to write, but the people who graciously gave their time and energy in sharing the loss of their loved ones kept me motivated. I am indebted to Doug, Regi, and Jacob Watt, Becky Pines, Ken Slaught, Todd Dean, Margaret Snyder, Clarise Brady, Chuck and Loretta Ricciardi, Dr. Randi McAllister, Bill Chadwick, Dr. Cendra Lynn of Griefnet, Kevin Grant, PJ Kerr, and Dean Lies. Your willingness to help other people, your enthusiasm, humor (yes, humor!), and your belief in this project made its completion possible. All of you took a simple idea and helped create a needed tool for families who are—or will someday go—where you have been. Your courage amazes me. Thank you.

Also, special thanks to my father, Joseph O'Connor Jr., who provided many insights and helpful thoughts from his work with grieving families for over thirty-five years. Thanks to my brother, Neil, and brother-in-law, Chuck, for their insights on understanding the funeral process.

Finally, a heartfelt and loving thank you to my wonderful wife, Krista, for your constant encouragement and belief in me. And thanks to my beautiful children, Janae, Ellie, and Joseph. Your surprise attacks on the cookie jar in my office are blessed interruptions. The sounds of your little feet on my hardwood floor are pitter-patters of life.

Introduction

A hundred years from now, it will not matter what my bank account was, the sort of house I lived in, or the kind of car I drove. But the world may be different because I was important in the life of a child.

                                          Author unknown

If we are going to speak to our children about matters of life and faith, then we must talk to them about the reality of death. That's the premise of this book. It's that simple. While most of us would probably agree that it's important to prepare our children for every aspect of life, the thought of talking to them about funerals, death, and the life beyond goes down like castor oil. I've never drunk castor oil, but I've seen enough *Little Rascals* reruns to know that the stuff made Alfalfa's ears twitch. I've also been to a number of funerals and I know what those did to me.

Talking about funerals, death, and the life beyond is like that. It makes us twitch. It startles us. Becky Pines, whose story you'll read about later, said it best: "When someone you love dies, it even hurts to breathe." When we try to talk honestly with one another and our children about our dreams and hopes of the life beyond, we get lockjaw. We live, but we don't know how to die. We don't know what to say about death because it is something we don't want to experience. Not in our loved one's lives. Not in our lives.

And so, I offer you this book. It's a start.

This book is written for you and your children. Your nieces and nephews. Your grandchildren. The children you work with. It is a book about being honest. It is a book that asks more questions than it answers. It is a book that does not present the final word but initiates a conversation on a difficult subject most people prefer to avoid.

This is a book about hope.

It is not a book about theology. It is about people like you and me struggling to figure out what they really believe when the unbelievable has happened. And then wondering, "What in the world am I going to say to my kids? How am I going to explain what just happened in our family and what I believe about the God who saw this whole thing happen?"

The foundation of this book is faith. In examining the deepest questions of life and death, we either choose to live by faith or, when we look at the other limited options around us, we are ultimately left with despair. If our children are to pass on the Christian faith to their children in a very real and relevant way, it must be a faith grounded in hope. Nowhere is a stronger hope to be found than in the secure knowledge and love of God. Who, then, can lead us to this understanding of God?

A curious snapshot of the life beyond—God's eternal kingdom—depicts children leading wild animals in a world conspicuously absent of adults. "The wolf will live with the lamb, the leopard will lie down with the goat, the calf and the lion and the yearling together; and a little child will lead them. The cow will feed the bear, their young will lie down together, and the lion will eat straw like the ox. The infant will play near the hole of the cobra, and the young child put his hand into the viper's nest. They will neither harm nor destroy on all my holy mountain, for the earth will be full of the knowledge of the LORD as the waters cover the sea" (Isa. 11:6–9).

Hmmm...makes you wonder, doesn't it? Children, God's fingerpainting of innocence and trust, stand near the summit of God, a safe place free of harm or destruction. It is, perhaps, from this perspective that we can begin to tackle this dangerous animal of death and dying while still here on earth.

Inside these pages, you'll find a few of my own personal experiences with funerals and death, but more importantly, you will meet a number of my friends and family who have walked the road you are now on. I hope they become your friends. I hope their stories give you the hope you need to make it through to tomorrow. And maybe you just might feel the tug of a little hand leading you along the way.

1

Walking through the Shadowlands

Preparing Your Child for All of Life and Death

I'm not afraid to die . . . I just don't want to be there when it happens.

Woody Allen

I was drained. Exhausted. Only a few days earlier, my wife, Krista, had received an unexpected phone call informing us that one of my former students had drowned in a tragic boating accident on the Sacramento River Delta. As it is for everyone involved in a sudden death, especially accidents like this one, the next few days were physically, emotionally, mentally, and spiritually draining. Death has a reckless tendency to sap our every available resource.

Only nineteen years old, Joel was one of three tall, strapping brothers. Jacob, Joel, and Jeremiah Watt had all been involved in our youth ministry at one time or another during the previous five years. Doug and Regi, Joel's parents, had invited Krista and me on numerous water-skiing trips. We were friends with the family, and they were big supporters in our work with teenagers. On my last water-skiing trip with the Watt family to the Colorado River, I remember Joel and Jeremiah futilely attempting to teach me how to play Solitaire. I was never any good at cards, but like the Watt family, I loved to water-ski.

Every year the Watt family and dozens of family friends met at the Sacramento River Delta for a couple of weeks of water-skiing, jet-skiing, wave-running, lying in the baking sun, and enjoying sizzling barbeques during the cool, star-filled nights. With its long-'n'-lazy hot summer days, slow golden sunsets, and perfect early-morning glassy water, the Delta is one of the most wonderful places on God's incredible earth to kick back and relax. Every year, the Watt family looked forward to leaving Southern California and getting back up to the Delta.

Late in the afternoon of July 23, 1993, Joel and his girlfriend, Andrea, hopped into a sleek fiberglass competition raceboat piloted by an older man and his wife. In its earlier days, the raceboat had been used in the Pacific Ocean to run back and forth between Catalina Island and Los Angeles. Fiberglass raceboats like this one take a tremendous pounding from the random, bobbing movement of the ocean waves. However, before being put into racing retirement, the fiberglass hull had been reinforced and the boat was now used to speed along the smooth, mirror-like waters of the Delta.

When Joel and Andrea jumped into the boat, neither of them even thought to put on a life jacket. *A life jacket?* They were just going for a quick spin before dinner and would be back in a few minutes.

The sleek boat raced along the Delta's glassy waters. With the warm, late-afternoon wind whipping their hair, Joel and Andrea never realized that this would be their last moment spent together. They had dated for over a year, and had even talked about getting married someday.

Putting slowly across the wide, dark blue span of the Delta's waters, a lumbering cabin cruiser generated a large, but inconspicuous wake. Zipping across the water's smooth surface at approximately sixty miles an hour, the raceboat and its four occupants approached the wake like a buzz saw ready to cut through a twig. This high-performance boat had powered its way through race after race in heavy surf conditions; it wouldn't even feel this three-foot wake.

At the precise split second the raceboat came down upon the wake, something went radically wrong underneath the bottom of the boat. Disintegrating into hundreds of fragmented pieces, the reinforced hull blew apart in an explosive spray of fiberglass and water. The boat split in half. Joel, who happened to be sitting in the back of the boat, was hurled forward into the deck face first. The tremendous force-filled impact knocked him unconscious. In a splashing flurry of sharp fiberglass shards, Joel, Andrea, the boat driver, and his wife were catapulted out of the flying wreckage, their bodies launching chaotically in every direction.

Witnessing this unbelievable crash, nearby boats raced over to the wreckage and the injured bodies floating in the water. One. Two. Three. Andrea, the boat driver, and his wife were quickly pulled out of the murky Delta water. Within a few minutes, the rescuers discovered that a fourth person had also been in the boat but was nowhere to be found. Radio calls for help were quickly made and the injured threesome were sped off to the nearest marina to meet awaiting paramedics.

With every life-giving second ticking away, volunteer rescuers continued their frantic search for Joel in the immediate area surrounding the boat crash. Divers were called in from the sheriff's department. Doug, Regi, and the rest of the vacationing group were notified of the boat crash and Joel's disappearance. Prayers went up immediately. Some of the vacationers tore off to the hospital; others waited at the marina. Hoping. Praying their worst fear would not be realized. It all seemed so unreal. Could it really be happening?

After a few hours of diving and searching, Joel's lifeless body was finally found.

No More Tears in Heaven

In the immediate days that followed, I was asked to assist in preparing and leading Joel's memorial service. A few months earlier, I had performed a funeral service for a college student who fell to his death while rock climbing. Two young lives. Two accidental deaths.

I began to help Joel's family with the details of his memorial service. Friends and family members were interviewed to get personal glimpses and experiences of favorite memories with Joel. Music was selected. Best friends and close family members were asked to share a few thoughts and feelings about Joel's life. Joel's father, Doug, and a family friend created a wonderful slide show of Joel's life with Eric Clapton's hit song, "Tears in Heaven."

On the day of Joel's memorial service, over six hundred adults and young people came to celebrate the life God gave Joel and to mourn the tragic loss they felt at his death. As emotionally wrenching and sad as it was, Joel's memorial service was also punctuated with moments of laughter and lighthearted memories as people recounted the fun times they had had with him. The memorial service was painful and was in no way designed to deny the sadness felt by everyone, but celebrating Joel's life with a few timely moments of laughter had a soothing and refreshing way of flushing out the deep currents of grief and desperate pain felt on the inside. As tears were a welcome guest, so was laughter.

For anyone close to the person (or to the family members) who has died, funerals are an exhausting process of pain, disbelief, sobbing, anger, sadness, and every other imaginable, combustible, roller-coaster emotion thrown in. That's how I felt after Joel's memorial service as I flopped myself on our king-sized bed to spend a few quiet moments with my three-year-old daughter, Janae.

Death has a reckless tendency to sap our every available resource.

I was exhausted. Janae was filled with questions. As she asked me all sorts of questions about the boat accident and Joel's death, I thought to myself, *That's a good question! She's obviously quite interested in knowing more about death.* I offered a simple explanation of how Joel died and told her that he was now in heaven with Jesus. That wasn't enough.

"Where's heaven?" Janae asked.

Another good question.

In simple, easy-to-understand words, I told this insightful three-year-old with golden curls, "Well, I don't know exactly where heaven is, but I can tell you what heaven is like."

I then explained that the Bible promises heaven is a place where we get to live forever with the God who made us— that there is no death in heaven, no pain or ow-ees or bee stings or scraped knees, and finally, that there's no crying or tears in heaven because it is a wonderful, happy place with no problems or things to make us sad.

Janae's face turned pensive for a moment. She then tilted her head to one side and her face lit up with an "Aha!" light-bulb-clicking insight.

"Yeah," Janae beamed, "heaven's not a crying place."

Out of the mouths of babes . . . come book titles.

I quickly discovered that children, even toddlers, have much to teach us logical, objective, clinical, "all-knowing" adults about eternal matters. Though this book is written for adults and parents who want to teach, help, and guide children in understanding the sensitive issues surrounding death, dying, and eternal life, it's also written to serve as a catalyst for us BIG people to reflect upon how we live our lives. This book is for you as well as your children. It is written to help all of us live with the unpopular reality that we are in the process of dying. It's also written to remind us—or perhaps to explain for the very first time—that through Jesus Christ, we are in the process of living for eternity.

This isn't a morbid book about death. This is a book about life. We can't talk about death without talking about life, and we can't talk about life without talking about death. For right now, your kids and the children you know or work with have a lot of questions, and they just might be wondering if you're thinking what they're thinking.

Walking through the Shadowlands

Shadowlands, the movie about the life of C. S. Lewis and his late-in-life marriage to Joy Davidman, offers a gripping, emotional scene between Lewis and his young stepson, David. After his mother dies of cancer, David tucks himself away in Lewis's upper attic, near the old wooden wardrobe made famous in The Chronicles of Narnia. As David sits alone in tears grieving the death of his mother, Lewis quietly arrives at the top of the stairwell and moves to comfort him. The sweeping, gentle music in the soundtrack starts to build as Lewis puts his arms around the boy and begins to cry with him. Reaching a shuddering crescendo of emotion, both man and boy sob uncontrollably as they share the heavy burden of each other's tremendous grief. C. S. Lewis, a brilliant Christian scholar and world-renowned writer, is broken, becoming like a child earnestly and honestly exposing his vulnerable, wounded heart.

Sitting on a dusty wooden step holding one another, man and boy allow the raw force of their grief to explode wide open. This scene captures the essence of walking through the shadowlands of death together. There are no pious, spiritual Band-Aid explanations for Joy's death by well-meaning family and friends. No one hands them a Kleenex to wipe away their tears. No one says, "I know just how you feel." There are no FTD flowers, no Hallmark sympathy cards, no casseroles or pots full of chicken soup, no long-winded messages left on the answering machine, no gifts, no Scripture verses, special songs, or grief counselor referrals. All you see and experience is horrible, holy grief. Pure and unadulterated pain. A man. A boy. In terrible agony. Bearing that pain together.

It was one of those rare Hollywood moments that reaches beyond the unreal and gently touches a very real part of everyone's soul. That's why there wasn't a dry eye in the audience. *Shadowlands* gave people permission to cry. It would have been very difficult to watch that scene without recalling and reliving (to some degree) the grief we've experienced over the death of a favorite grandparent, father, mother, child, coworker, or best friend. To say that the scene is "moving" or "powerful" isn't enough; you have to see it for yourself.

Not only did *Shadowlands* allow people to grieve and cry for the death of loved ones, it demonstrated dramatically the intimacy adults and children can experience when pain is shared. Over the past few years, there has been a significant increase in the number of movies dealing with the impact death has on friends and family members. To some degree, death is a reality Hollywood understands. Hollywood knows what sells movie tickets. Hollywood confronts us with what we are too afraid to face alone.

I'll never forget watching *Steel Magnolias* a few years ago on a flight home from Chicago. I didn't know a thing about the movie, so I wasn't exactly prepared to begin bawling my eyes out at thirty thousand feet. Just two months earlier, I had lost one of my best buddies to a four-year struggle with cancer. The last time I saw Dana Robinson was when he was lying semiconscious in his hospital bed surrounded by tons of tubes and machines. As a few of his close friends stood around his bed, his body began to shudder and shake with convulsions. Buzzers and alarms went off. The nurses cleared us out of the room. Dana went into a coma. Two days later, he died.

Exactly a week after Dana's death, Krista and I discovered that she was pregnant with our first child. That one week was a wild, whiplashing, stomach-busting roller coaster of life and death. So . . . in the movie, when the hospital scene comes along of the young husband signing the legal documents to disconnect Julia Roberts's comatose body from the life-support machines, I began to crumble over my salted peanuts and Diet Coke in a pathetic mess of tears and sorrow.

Seated next to me (also in tears) was another good friend of mine, Glen Davis. As I sat in my seat sobbing, Glen poked me in the ribs and said, "Keep watching . . . you have to watch this next scene," which just happened to be the funeral scene. As Sally Field walks with her friends among the marble and granite cemetery gravestones after her daughter's funeral, she launches through the emotional stratosphere in a fury of confusion, anger, sorrow, and pain. She is so distraught that there is nothing her friends can do to soothe her pain. It is painfully clear that she is deep in the shadowlands.

As Glen and I watched the cemetery scene, I'm sure the plane lost a couple thousand feet in altitude as we turned into a heavy pile of slobbering baggage. Emotional mush. With tears streaming down our faces, Glen and I shared the pain of Dana's death and the tremendous loss we felt. I couldn't help wondering what other people in the plane were thinking when they walked past Glen and me. *What is up with those two guys?* At that wonderful, vulnerable, very public moment of releasing the pent-up, poisonous pain out of our systems, we looked more like withering weeds than steel magnolias. But so what . . . it sure did feel good to cry!

Though Hollywood is giving America permission to cry (and probably saving people millions of dollars in counseling fees!), Hollywood cannot walk with our children through the intimidating shadowlands of pain and death. Whether you are sixty or six years old, the shadowlands is a scary place to enter all alone. Nobody wants to walk among the mountains of fear and the valleys of despair alone. If you don't walk, guide, instruct, and help your children through the shadowlands, who will? Yes, paying only seven bucks to sit in a dark theater to corporately grieve with hundreds of strangers vicariously experiencing the pain of actors on-screen is a pretty good deal for a one-time cry, but at best, it is thoroughly inadequate to deal with a child's important questions about life and death.

It would be presumptuous for me to assume I have profound answers to all your children's questions about life, death, and dying—the hows, the whys, and every exact detail of what happens after we die—because I don't. The purpose of this book is to honor and respond to children's honest questions about what happens when we die and acknowledge what we know to be God's promises for life after death. Children's questions are holy and innocent, and it is upon this sacred ground that I want to walk with sensitive bare feet. My hope is that you and I will be better equipped to walk with our children through the shadowlands. Or at least, that we will learn to stop dodging the shadows. We have the unique privilege of preparing our children for all events, surprises, circumstances, and special moments in life. That includes death and the awesome questions it raises. If we teach and model an understanding (however limited) and a willingness to talk about the whole of life and death with our children, we will arm them with a flashlight the Bible calls "wisdom." And kids love flashlights. Why? Because they're perfect for eliminating shadows.

King Solomon, the wisest, richest, most powerful man on earth at his time, a man intimately acquainted with every pleasure the world had to offer, wrote these sobering words for us to consider:

> It is better to go to a house of mourning
>   than to go to a house of feasting,
> for death is the destiny of every man;
>   the living should take this to heart.

> Sorrow is better than laughter,
>   because a sad face is good for the heart.
> The heart of the wise is in the house of mourning,
>   but the heart of fools is in the house of pleasure.
> Ecclesiastes 7:2–4

If it is indeed true that we are wiser to enter the house of mourning instead of hitting the block party down the street, why, then, are we so reluctant and ill equipped to talk about death and eternal matters with our children? How is it that we live in one of the most progressive, powerful, technologically advanced societies on earth, but we stumble and stutter talking about something we know we must all face one day? Why is there such an inner and cultural resistance to confronting the personal pain and volatile emotions provoked deep within our spirits when someone we love dies? Why do blank stares shroud our faces and words never get past our lips when our children ask us if Grandma died? What pain are we hiding that motivates us to lie outright to our children when someone dies? What burden will our children someday bear when they confront the hidden, ugly emotions they were taught to stuff, deny, avoid, and hide when a very special person they loved died?

Yes, these are difficult, sensitive, challenging, and soul-stirring questions. They're questions we'd rather deny or just pretend don't exist. Like our shadow, these are questions that simply won't disappear.

If you're feeling perplexed, confused, intimidated, or scared about talking to your children about life and death, be assured that you're not alone. Many parents feel the same way. By the time you finish the next chapter, you'll be equipped and prepared to talk to your child about this important subject. You just may surprise yourself by discovering the "D-word" is easier to talk about than you previously thought.

2

The D-Word, Your Kids, and What You Can Do about It

Giving Your Child the Straight Scoop on Life and Death

Children enter school as question marks and leave as periods.

Neil Postman

When I first began this project, my original intention was to write a book encouraging parents to be proactive in talking to their children about a very difficult subject. I quickly discovered that nobody wants to be proactive with something that hurts, wounds, and steals. I'd venture to say that most conversations about death between parents and their kids, if they happen at all, occur as a result of a death in the family and not the foresight of proactive parenting. The conversation with my daughter in chapter 1 grew out of crisis and tragedy—*not proactive parenting*. I can't hold you to a different standard. Most of us don't live that way. I don't live that way.

You've most likely picked up this book or received it as a gift because of a recent death of someone close to you and your children. The death of a mom. A dad. A grandparent. A classmate. Family friend. Coworker. Neighbor. Even a pet. Besides trying to deal with your own pain and grief from losing a loved one, your kids are probably asking you questions like:

- "How come Grandma never comes over anymore?"
- "Mommy, why is my goldfish floating at the top of the bowl?"
- "What's a funeral? Why are we going to one today?"
- "How come Mommy is so sick? Why doesn't she play with me anymore?"
- "Billy told me his cousin died in an accident. Are you going to die too?"
- "If God loves us so much, why does he let people die?"
- "What is heaven like? Where is heaven, anyway?"
- "Daddy, I'm scared to die. I don't ever want you or me or Mommy to die."
- "I miss Grandpa. Can I call him today?"
- "Mommy, why are you crying so much? You never cried like this before."
- "I don't want to go to Aunt Sue's for two weeks. I want to stay with you!"
- "I'm so mad at God! Why did he take my little sister away?"

So what can you say when your kids ask you about the "D-word"? How can you help them understand what death is without confusing them? How do you deal with all the other questions that quickly follow: Did Grandpa die in pain? Where is my mommy now? What is a funeral? Can I go to heaven to visit my baby sister?

Dealing with the D-Word

You can deal with the D-word by giving your child simple and clear explanations of what death is. That's what this chapter is all about—discussing death as a physical reality in the natural order of how things work here on planet earth. If we can first talk with our children about death as a physical reality, we can then move forward by explaining what our faith has to say about it. Chapter 3 ventures into the spiritual aspects of death.

When a loved one dies, one of the most common responses of a grieving child or adult is to simply want their mother, father, brother, sister, grandparent, or friend back.

If you're dealing with the very recent death of a family member or loved one, you will probably revisit this discussion in a number of different ways over the coming weeks, months, and years. You, your children, and your family may still be in shock over what's just happened. When a loved one dies, one of the most common responses of a grieving child or adult is to simply want their mother, father, brother, sister, grandparent, or friend back. Though your children may not completely understand your explanations of death because of the shock of what has just occurred, it is an important first step.

Let me take a wild guess at some of the things running through your head. First, you're probably saying, "I know talking to my kids about death is important, but I'm scared! I don't know how to answer all of their questions. I don't want to scare them. What if I mess up? How am I supposed to answer the 'why' questions? What if I make things worse? I have three kids ages ten, seven, and five . . . do I talk to them together or individually? How can I talk to my kids when I'm trying to deal with my own pain and grief?"

Good questions.

If you're someone who makes no particular claim to faith and does not have a religious affiliation, you may be asking questions along these lines: "I consider myself spiritual, but I'm finding it difficult to explain what I believe to my kids. I don't even believe in God . . . what am I supposed to say when my son asks me about heaven? I'm not even certain what I believe, so how can I help my kids when they ask such difficult questions?" Those are important questions. We will deal with them in the next chapter. For right now, let's deal with death itself and how you can talk to your children about it.

Helping Children Understand Death

Here are a number of simple explanations to help your children understand what death is and what it is not. As you'll see, the following information makes no religious references to God, heaven, hell, streets of gold, angels, or pearly gates. The goal here is to provide clarity about what death is in order to prevent confusion between faith and death.

Death is not sleeping. When we die, our bodies do not work anymore. When we go to sleep, our bodies are still working and we wake up. When we die, our bodies don't wake up. We don't eat, sleep, or play anymore. We can't because our bodies no longer work.

Death is not a long trip. Despite what Aunt Mabel might have said, death is not a long trip or vacation. If we go on vacation, we always return home. Once we die, we never come back. We are buried in the ground, above the ground, or our bodies are burned to ashes. Long trips are usually fun adventures. Death is not fun like a long trip.

Death is not temporary. Death lasts forever. Though it may be hard for you to understand what "forever" means, when something dies, it is dead for always. If a bird dies, it can't wake up again. It is dead forever. When we die, our physical bodies are dead forever.

Death is not just for old people. People of all ages die. Babies die. Children die. Teenagers die. Adults die. It's true that old people die, but they don't die just because they're old. Old people die, like everyone else, because their bodies stop working.

Death is not just for bad guys. On TV, it often seems like just the bad guys die. In real life, everybody dies. That means good guys and bad guys. Good people die and bad people die. Most of the time, it is impossible to know when it is our time to die.

Death is not just for bugs and animals. Bugs die, animals die, and even people die. It's easy to find dead bugs in your house or backyard. It's also common to see dead animals like squirrels, deer, or coyotes along the side of the road. When we see dead bugs and animals, we are reminded that all living things will one day die.

Death is not a punishment. When someone we love dies, it is not because they were being punished or because *you* are being punished. Nothing you did or did not do made the person die. Even though death can make you feel very bad inside, death is never a punishment. Just as everyone in this world is born, everyone also dies.

Death is not funny or fake. If you watch a lot of violent TV shows or movie videos, you'll probably see a lot of people die. All of these people who pretend to die are actors and actresses. Their deaths are fake; sometimes, their deaths are even made to seem funny. In real life, death is real. It is never funny or fake.

Everyone who is sick does not die. There is a big difference between someone who is sick and someone who has died *because of being sick*. Just as there is a big difference between warm bathwater and boiling hot water on the stove, some sicknesses are much worse than others. If you or I have a cold, it is very unlikely that we would die from it. Everyone gets sick, but not everyone dies from being sick.

Death is not an easy subject to talk about. Death upsets people in all sorts of different ways and many people are scared to talk about it. It is difficult for people to honestly express their feelings about death. Some people like to talk about a loved who died because it helps them. For others, this is very difficult. We should not criticize people who do not want to talk about death or their feelings about a loved one who has died.

A Nation in Denial

Regardless of your faith tradition or personal beliefs, if you find it difficult to talk with your kids about funerals, death, and the life beyond, you're not alone. You are a part of a society that ignores death and does not know how to talk about it. *This is not your fault.* You live in a postmodern culture that is devoid of rich tradition, has few meaningful rituals, and lacks a common language for discussing eternal matters.

> *You are a part of a society that ignores death and does not know how to talk about it.*

In America, we embrace living and resist dying. We are not very good mourners. We like to pride ourselves on being a nation of winners, but death means that we lose. Big time. We are a society confused about matters of life and death.

In many ways, we are a nation in denial. Our culture is not sure when life begins or when it ends.

For the majority of American society, the mourning rituals are gone. Black attire is out. Funerals are tense, stiff, often unemotional affairs. The object, it seems, is not to cry. Little thought or creativity is put into memorial services. Where are our requiems? Where is our wailing? Why don't we shout, scream, and shake our fists, demanding an answer for the death of our loved ones? When someone we love dies, we die. Death is not a solitary experience. Yet our culture would prefer to keep it that way. Friends and relatives are in awe of the parent or spouse who seems to be "so strong." Strength is admired and weakness is disdained. This American cloak of silence and denial makes it difficult to talk with one another and our children about living and dying.

If a loved one of yours has recently died and you have found that family members, friends, members of your church, and even the pastoral staff lack the resources and compassionate understanding to help you in your suffering, you're not alone. Though many mainline denominations and smaller independent churches have wonderful grief counseling and healing ministries, the church as a whole has been heavily influenced by our culture's reticence in talking about life and death. Yes, even in the church, we aren't very good at understanding death and those around us who are grieving.

In the Christian faith, we have a theology that is centered around the central themes of life and death. Death is seen as a door. We go from life to life through death. But we talk a lot about life and not enough about death. If we were really honest, those of us in the church would have to admit that we find it much easier to talk about resurrection and eternal life than we do about suffering and death. It's okay to talk about Jesus' death, but not our own. Our own death is a little too close to home.

Honest Shock

As a college student, I often worked at my father's mortuary when I was home on break. To make much-needed cash, my time was usually spent gardening, painting, delivering flowers to the cemetery, and helping out with other odd jobs around the O'Connor Laguna Hills Mortuary. On one occasion, my father asked me to do a simple task that I'll never forget.

While standing in the back parking lot, he asked me to give him a hand taking a casket out of the brown funeral hearse. As he opened the back door, the wheeled casket holder called a "church truck" was set in place. Inside the hearse was a pink casket with a beautiful bouquet of flowers on top. When he asked me to wheel the casket into the mortuary chapel, I inquired who was inside. His reply?

"A sixteen-year-old girl. She died in a car accident."

As I slowly began pushing the pink casket toward the side door of the chapel, I thought, *Here I am pushing the casket of a sixteen-year-old girl.*

I stopped with an uncomfortable mix of terrified wonder and dread.

She's dead.

For a few brief moments, I couldn't get over the shocking reality before me. The pink casket contained the lifeless body of a young teenage girl. Death, lying right before me, made me stop and think. *This is final. She is gone.*

As the son of a mortician, I have had the opportunity to make a number of observations about how people understand and deal with death. Though I do not claim to be an expert about death and dying, I'd venture to say that more time is spent after funerals talking about how wonderful the salmon cheese dip is than any personal feelings about what was said, felt, or experienced at the funeral itself. Most of the time, we are in honest shock. Death has taken someone away from us whom we loved and adored. We don't know what to say. It seems like there's nothing to say. We fear that others will think of us as weak or morbid for bringing the subject up, and since death is already a taboo subject, we quickly hurry back to our busy lives in the hope that we're not next. Death is like a big "Do Not Touch" sign we are afraid to approach. But if we are to be a help to our children, we must be willing to face the truth about death.

The Truth about Death

One of the most practical ways to help your kids deal with the D-word is to face the truth of your own feelings about death and the life beyond. Once you've searched your heart about how you really feel, you may find it easier to verbalize your thoughts and feelings with your kids.

You may be tempted to believe that it's not a good idea to be vulnerable and show your own hurt, pain, and tears to your kids because you want to "be strong" for them. But it's easy for kids to mistake strength as indifference. Silence can be a seedbed for doubt and insecurity. There's a place for strength and a place for being honest with your emotions. You'll find stories in this book from others who have learned the importance of balancing strength and vulnerability with their kids. Remember: Kids learn to emulate not only their parents' actions and words but also their parents' handling of emotions.

It is quite unlikely that you ever had a part-time job working at a mortuary. However, you probably have some very definite thoughts and feelings about death. I believe that every casket or box of ashes contains a number of truths about what we've all thought about death at one time or another. Do these thoughts sound familiar?

We don't like death. Sounds simple, but in order to face the reality of death, we need to admit how we really feel about it. Who likes death? Right now, you may be going through a tremendously difficult experience because of the death of someone you love. It's painful. Confusing. For some, physically debilitating. It is an unbelievable experience that is punctured with the truth that what is happening to you and your family is actually real. Even though it is normal to go through a period of denial when a death occurs, it is necessary to accept your feelings about death in order to help your children explore their thoughts and feelings about what is happening in their lives.

We don't want to die. Not only do you and I not like death, we also don't want to die. Here we have two distinct realities: First, we don't like death because of the troublesome feelings it stirs inside of us when a loved one dies. And second, the deaths of those around us remind us of the fact that our own death is only a matter of time. *Literally.* Death rips the lid off any sense of permanence we have in our lives. Death is a little *too* final and we don't like that one bit. Though there are those few brave Christian souls, existential stalwarts, or macho *Die Hard* Bruce Willis types who cry, "I'm not afraid to die," most of us know we don't want to die. In one way or another, we are all afraid to die. If you don't like to talk about death with your kids, your spouse, or your close friends, it's probably because deep down inside, you don't want to die. If that's one of your fears, relax . . . you're normal.

We don't like unfinished business. Let me simply state a truth about the human heart: We don't like unfinished business. Death reminds us of the things we wish we would have said, the promises we made to ourselves, and the hurts of broken relationships. Death whispers the regrets of unfinished business. It's uncomfortable and painful to explore the areas in our lives that we wish would have been cleared up long ago. That's another reason why we clam up when a death occurs.

If you can begin to explore your own feelings and experiences with death and loss, you are well on your way to building a bridge to your child's heart. There's nothing easy about talking to your children about funerals, death, and the life beyond, but you cannot hurt or injure your child by honestly answering their questions in a sensitive and loving way to the best of your ability. Silence hurts. Caring conversations can help ease the pain of loss.

Before we look at how to teach your children a number of spiritual principles about life and death in the next chapter, here are a few solid ways to prepare yourself to talk to your kids about the D-word.

- Examine your previous experiences with death. What stories might be appropriate to share with your children? How can your story help them?
- If a death has recently happened, ask yourself, "What have my children been told or not been told about the death? What questions have my kids asked that have not been answered? What kind of misinformation about the death needs to be corrected?"
- Take your children's ages into consideration. Use simple, age-appropriate words and concepts to answer their questions. (We'll examine this subject in later chapters.)
- If someone in your family is terminally ill, assess the current situation. Enlist the support of your pastor, priest, or minister as well as hospital support groups or social workers. They may have resources that will be helpful to you and your family. Have the children been told about the illness and the probable death of your loved one?
- Talk to someone with children who has had a similar experience. Ask them what worked in speaking to their children about the death of a loved one.
- Call a family grief counselor. There are county agencies, hospitals, and churches who provide bereavement counseling and support.

- Talk with your spouse and develop a simple plan to talk with your children.
- As much as possible, find a time and place free of distraction. Take the phone off the hook before you sit down to talk with your kids.

Prepare to build a bridge of hope.

3

A Bridge of Hope

Building Heaven in Your Child's Heart

> Think of yourself as a seed patiently wintering in the earth;
> waiting to come up a flower in the Gardener's good time, up
> into the real world, the real waking. I suppose that our whole
> present life, looked back from there, will seem only a drowsy
> half-waking.
>
> C. S. Lewis

*I*n the hit children's movie *A Little Princess*, Sara Crewe is
the delightful and beloved daughter of an English military
officer. When her father is sent off to war in Europe, Sara is
sent to the strict New York boarding school her mother attended as a young girl. Led by the cruel headmistress, Miss
Minchin, this rigid boarding school is nothing like the en-
chanting adventures Sara shared with her father when they
lived in the mysterious land of India.

Though at first she's an outsider, Sara earns the respect of
her peers through her enchanted, passionate stories of
princes and princesses, romance, danger, and faraway lands.

She rescues them from the dangers of conformity, monotony, and boarding school boredom. These girls were waiting to be freed from the dark monotony of Miss Minchin's legalistic rule; they were waiting for a story to be told, something that would capture their minds and seize their hearts with passion. And Sara delivered in a grand way.

Sara Crewe offered her classmates the one thing her boarding school could not—hope. In the midst of a very cold and rigid learning environment, Sara's colorful storytelling awakened a spark of life in each one of the girls' hearts.

Despite the tyranny of a cruel headmistress, Sara's imagination helped build a bridge of hope for her young friends who were trapped in a chasm of despair. When the tyranny of death strikes our home, all of us could use someone like Sara Crewe.

Adults are in the unique position to respond to children's questions about heaven and the life beyond by building a bridge of hope in their children's hearts. This bridge of hope is founded upon the life, death, and resurrection of Jesus Christ. Hope, above all else, is the Christian distinctive.

In the last chapter we discussed the importance of talking clearly to children about the physical reality of death. The next logical step is to explore what the Christian faith tradition says about the spiritual nature of life and death. This is where parents get stumped. This is where I got stumped!

Death forces the question, "What do you believe?"

When Janae asked me about the physical details surrounding Joel Watt's death (how the accident happened, who was in the boat, what the memorial service was like, and so on), I wasn't very well prepared. And then she pulled a double whammy by asking me questions of a spiritual nature.

Telling our children about death is one thing, but communicating what we believe about the spiritual nature of life and death makes us scratch and squirm as if someone dumped itching powder down our backs. Why?

Death rips at the anchors of what we believe and pulls at the core values of who we are.

A deep sense of loss, abandonment, and injustice can drown us in a sea of despair, making our faith seem irrelevant and useless.

The agony of losing a loved one can make us scream at God, "This wasn't part of the deal!"

Death forces the question, "What do you believe?"

What are you supposed to say when your children ask you, "Why did God let this happen?" if you don't know yourself?

This was the inner conflict Todd Dean faced with his son and daughter when his wife, Charlotte, died of cancer. His dilemma may be remarkably similar to what you are going through right now. Listen to what he has to say to parents who are trying to reconcile the tragedy of death, their personal faith in God, and the faith they are trying to pass on to their children: "How do you comfort your children with 'God loves you. He'll take care of us,' when you're wondering, 'Where is God?' When a person's faith is shattered by the death of a loved one, the last thing they want to do is feel like a hypocrite with their children. Death definitely produces a lot of cognitive dissonance with our faith and how we communicate that faith to our children. This is what makes so many parents scared to talk to their kids."

As Todd and I talked about this tension felt by many grieving parents in one of our numerous conversations, he offered these suggestions: "Death is a time for regrouping and self-assessment. Before talking to your kids, you need to ask yourself, 'What do I believe? How did I get here? Where is my hope?' Those are difficult questions, but it's necessary for parents to think about them and come to their own conclusions about their beliefs. How else can we talk honestly with our kids?"

It's Okay to Hurt

Before we look at some simple and practical ways to communicate what we believe to our children, I want to take a moment to say that it's okay to hurt. I hope that doesn't sound too trite or simplistic for what you're experiencing right now, but many people don't allow themselves to feel the immensity of their pain and loss. They think they should be stronger. Losing a loved one is a devastating loss for you and your family. You may be feeling a fury of volatile emotions like doubt, anger, denial, hopelessness, despair, sadness, and shock. You may be scared and worried about what to say or not to say to your kids. Even this book may be raising all sorts of uneasy questions you haven't thought about for a long while. Despite what anyone says, nobody knows what you are going through. Friends and family may share your pain, but they can't feel what you feel in your heart. Your pain is yours alone and it's okay to hurt. You are not a hypocrite for hurting.

If death has cast a dark shadow on the light of your faith, don't worry. Your struggle to believe is itself a sign of faith. Even if you're angry at God or feeling terribly separated from him, that too is a sign of faith. Give yourself some space. If you want to give your children the comfort, assurance, and hope of your faith even when you feel like your world has imploded—that, my friend, is real faith. You are not a hypocrite for hurting. You are not a hypocrite for sharing what you believe even if you're not sure of what you believe anymore. If there is a wide gulf between your faith and feelings right now because of the hurt and pain you are feeling, that's not hypocrisy... that's honesty. As you continue reading through this book, allow yourself to experience a wave of different emotions. You're human and it's okay to hurt. Honest.

Caution! Handle Heaven with Care

When a loved one dies, it's easy for children to confuse death and the spiritual concepts explained by adults. Why? Because children accept what adults say letter by letter and word for word. By separating the actual details of a death from the spiritual concepts, this confusion can often be eliminated.

Death is handled as death.

Faith is handled as faith.

In this way, children can learn about the reality of death and the circumstances regarding a particular death without jumping to incorrect religious assumptions. And, more importantly, they won't be put in a position to believe something that is not true. By separating these complicated subjects, adults can save children from spending years untangling sticky webs of misinformation about life, death, and matters of faith. They won't have to "unlearn" anything.

Helping children understand the reality of death and shaping their hearts for heaven is a delicate process. Let's look at how easily a child's understanding of heaven can be confused by the words she hears.

- One mother, whose baby died of SIDS, explained to her daughter that God took the baby away so he could sing in the angels' choir on Christmas Day. At first, the little girl was very angry at God for taking the baby away. And later, on Christmas Day, she was heartbroken that her baby brother was not singing in the choir at church.[1]
- After her mother's death, three-year-old Sarah Dean hopped on an airplane with her older brother and fa-

ther to visit relatives back East. Not only was Sarah extremely excited to be on an airplane for the first time, she was also thrilled to have the opportunity to see her mommy. As the plane flew through the clouds, she exclaimed to her daddy, "We're going to see Mommy." You see, Sarah understands heaven to be "up in the air where the clouds are." Her mommy is in heaven. The clouds are up in heaven. Therefore, by riding in an airplane through the clouds, she will be able to see her mommy in heaven.

Makes sense, doesn't it? It does for a three-year-old, but imagine how devastated Sarah would have been if Todd hadn't taken a few minutes to truthfully explain that Sarah wouldn't be able to see her mommy. As painful as that conversation was, Todd prevented what could have amounted to years of misunderstanding and confusion.

Teaching Your Child What the Bible Says about Life and Death

Sara Crewe told her friends fascinating stories. There is another story that offers a compelling theme of hope for everyone willing to be awakened from within. For every individual and every family who has searched for meaning, fulfillment, and a bridge of hope to cross the chasm of death, the story of God's unending love found in the Bible speaks to the deepest longings of the human heart. It offers a consistent, compelling theme of God's plan of redemption for all humankind. It is also unmistakably clear on the perplexing subject of death. Not only does it speak plainly and boldly about death, it also offers comfort and compassion for the dying.

Like Sara's vivid storytelling, the Bible offers a clear ray of hope in the midst of the tumultuous, dark emotions of grief. It doesn't dismiss the blinding emotions of anger, bitterness, guilt, confusion, remorse, or despair as unholy, unspiritual, or threatening to the honor of God. The Bible delivers a solid and secure confidence for the troubles and uncertainties we face each day. Through the grace of God, it offers the hope and certainty of heaven in this uncertain world.

Here are a number of practical ideas to start teaching your children what the Bible says about life and death. Whether or not your family is in crisis right now, these suggestions will help build a spiritual foundation for talking to your children about this important subject.

Begin with a Story

Kids love stories. Walk into any Christian bookstore and you'll find dozens of children's Bibles, bedtime devotionals, prayer books, storybooks with Bible themes, and Bible activity books. My kids' favorites are the *Eager Reader Bible* and devotional and *Little Visits with God*. These books are filled with creatively written Bible stories, age-appropriate questions, and clever scenarios. Teaching your children easy-to-understand Bible stories imprints faith impressions on their hearts through an activity they love. Reading Bible stories to your children at bedtime provides the opportunity to explore their questions about life and death. It also meets their need for security and nurturing by closing their day with you.

Bible Videos

Like books, Bible videos are a wonderful way to teach biblical principles to your kids. The stories of creation, Adam and Eve, Abraham, Moses and the Israelites, David and Goliath, and the life of Jesus are all great ways to teach and reinforce your family's faith tradition. Kids will watch these videos over and over.

Kids' Sing-a-Long Praise CDs

Our family has logged thousands of miles in our car with kids' praise songs that tell about God, famous Bible characters, and the situations of everyday life. Tapes like *Tiny Tot Pwaise* and the Focus on the Family's *Adventures in Odyssey* are incredibly useful and relevant to your child's growing faith. You'll even find yourself humming these songs when your kids aren't in the car.

Children's Books on Death and Grief

Not only do you want to use appropriate children's books to teach your children about your faith tradition, you'll also want to select books that talk about what happens when we die and what our heart feels when someone close to us dies. This is where books dealing with terminal illness, dying, and grief are essential in helping children process what they are feeling and experiencing. Go to a Christian bookstore, library, or bereavement organization to find helpful books and literature. The Compassionate Friends (see appendix B) has an excellent reading list for adults and children. Contact them for more information.

Ask Questions

Books, videos, and music tapes are helpful tools for helping children learn about faith, hope, love, God, life, death, and eternity, but never underestimate the power of a simple question. Questions are launch pads for igniting stimulating talks between you and your kids. Particularly for older kids and teenagers, asking relevant questions about their faith in God, their understanding of a particular Bible passage, or their everyday concerns is a sure way to earn their trust and confidence in you. Here is a list of simple questions to help you talk with your children about spiritual matters. Have fun with these questions. Create some of your own. Have a children's Bible handy to read a story related to your discussion. Depending on the age of your children, you may have to tweak some of these questions.

What is heaven? What does it mean to live forever?

What does the Bible say about death?

Who were Adam and Eve? What did they do wrong?

Why did Jesus come to earth? What did Jesus do when he was here?

Why did Jesus die on a cross?

What happened after Jesus was buried for three days?

What is prayer? Why do we pray to God? What do you pray for?

What does the Bible say about God's love? How does God love you?

What is sin? Why does sin make God sad?

What is forgiveness? What happens when we say "sorry" to God?

What is the church?

What do you think happens when we die?

What does the Bible say about heaven?

How do we know God loves us when we are sad?

Find a Really Good Sunday School

There are Sunday schools and then there are really *good* Sunday schools. Depending on your faith tradition or religious affiliation, your options may be limited. Try to find a Sunday school program for which your kids can't wait to wake up in the morning. I knew our children definitely had a really good Sunday school experience when one of my daughters woke up during the middle of the week and asked, "Is it time for Sunday school?" She'd ask my wife and me that question three to four times a week! Involving your children in a Sunday school program that they enjoy strengthens the values you are teaching at home. It also provides you another avenue for asking your children what they are learning about God, heaven, Bible stories, this life, and anything else that pops into their minds.

Create Your Own Family Faith Traditions

Some denominations have liturgical calendars that are perfect for enhancing the faith development of families throughout the year. The Advent (Christmas) and Lenten (Easter) seasons are great times to develop your own family faith traditions. Also, look for different times during the month or calendar year to develop meaningful times of talking, sharing, praying, reading Scripture, and encouraging one another as a family.

Talk about Suffering and Conflict

One of the most valuable things parents can teach their children is that life is difficult. Understanding suffering and its related emotions and learning how to handle conflict in healthy ways are critical life development skills. The Bible has a lot to say about pain and suffering in this life. Jesus himself said: "In this world you will have trouble. But take heart! I have overcome the world" (John 16:33). Suffering and death are as central to the Christian faith as resurrection and eternal life. As you teach your children what the Bible has to say about the struggles of this life, they will also learn that the Bible offers them hope and peace in the midst of their pain.

Talk about Sadness and Grief

The Bible is filled with examples of real people who experienced the terrible pain of grief. This is something every adult and child needs to know. Wander through Psalms and see how many passages are related to pain, anguish, suffering, mourning, and crying out to God. Ask yourself and your children, "Isn't this what we're feeling right now?" Study the lives of popular Bible characters and how they endured through their struggles and sadness. Read about when Jesus wept at the death of his friend Lazarus in John 11:1–44. Best of all, note that the Bible says times of sadness and grief are seasons that do not last forever. The pain you and your children are feeling will not always be as intense as it is right now.

Read about Heaven

At the end of the Bible in the Book of Revelation there is a beautiful description of heaven that you and your children can discuss together. Here, your children can learn that God "will wipe every tear from their eyes. There will be no more death or mourning or crying or pain, for the old order of things has passed away" (Rev. 21:4). See? Heaven's not a crying place! This is a promise for you and your kids!

Helping Your Children to Choose Life

Right now, you may be thinking that all of this is a bit overwhelming. Chances are your parents didn't communicate these concepts very well to you and you're wondering how in the world you're going to communicate them to your own children. Let me encourage you by saying that you don't have to be an expert to teach your children about life and death. You simply must be willing. And courageous.

When God finished giving the Old Testament law, his last words to the families of Israel were:

> Now what I am commanding you today is not too difficult for you or beyond your reach. It is not up in heaven, so that you have to ask, "Who will ascend into heaven to get it and proclaim it to us so we may obey it?" ... This day I call heaven and earth as witnesses against you that I have set before you life and death, blessings and curses. Now choose life, so that you and your children may live and that you may love the LORD your God, listen to his voice, and hold fast to him. For the LORD is your life ...
>
> Deuteronomy 30:11–12, 19–20

Talking to your children and raising them with an understanding of what God's Word says about life and death is not too difficult. It is not beyond your reach. You are simply helping your children to choose life. But it all begins with your decision as a parent to follow God's principles. Notice how God addresses parents first, "choose life, so that *you* and your children may live. . . ." Our spiritual development is directly related to our children's spiritual development. We can only create impressions of faith on their hearts if we are allowing God's Spirit to create faith impressions on our own hearts.

Helping your children choose life means making a simple commitment to take the time to talk with them about all of life and all of death. Or at least everything you know . . . that's a good enough place to start. It means taking the time to listen to their hurt and disappointment when their favorite pet dies. It means helping them identify the conflicting emotions they feel when faced with the loss of a mother, father, grandparent, sibling, or friend from school. It means taking the time to explain the foreign-sounding words and concepts of the funeral process they don't quite understand. It means looking for opportunities, perhaps as you're putting them down to bed, to explore a spontaneous question or curiosity about the mysteries and wonders of what happens when we die.

Helping your children choose life means making a simple commitment to take the time to talk with them about all of life and all of death.

These special, intimate moments are where memories are made, where impressions of faith are cemented upon our children's hearts forever. These are truths that are taught over a lifetime, not in a five-minute terse conversation aimed at finishing the subject so we don't have to bring it up again. They are critical family conversations that aren't left as the primary responsibility of the church to deal with in a fifteen-minute Sunday school lesson. These honest conversations about life and death are the building blocks of faith for our children. It is in learning, understanding, and following God's commands that lasting impressions of faith are made and choosing life is the most natural choice of all.

Helping your children choose life begins by simply telling them the truth.

4

Grandpa Did Not Go Away on a Long Trip

Telling Your Child the Truth about Death

Oh God, give me the courage to change the things I can change, the serenity to accept that which I cannot change, and the wisdom to distinguish between the two.

Thomas C. Hart

I was five years old when my grandmother Mimi died. My only memory of Mimi's death was the evening rosary service my family and I attended the night before her funeral. Though my father was a mortician, it was my first personal experience with death and the funeral process. I remember kneeling next to my father in the front row of the mortuary chapel for a long period of time. In front of us was Mimi's brown casket, the lid open and her body lying inside. As he knelt, my father was unusually quiet, his hands occasionally covering his face.

For a five-year-old, kneeling for long periods of time—except maybe in a sandbox—doesn't go over too well. I kept asking my father, "When are we going to go?" It was late. I was tired. I wanted my bed.

My father tells an interesting, completely different version of my experience of his mother's funeral. To prepare me for what was going to happen at Mimi's funeral, my father explained the burial process. "A grave," he said, "is the place where the casket is buried. The casket is the box that will hold Mimi's body." As any five-year-old might rhetorically ask, I said, "Are they going to put Mimi in a hole in the ground?"

After my grandmother's funeral service in Los Angeles the next day, our family headed to the cemetery for the graveside service. Much to my surprise, the cemetery was a beautiful place filled with sloping green hills, colorful flowers, ornate statues, American flags, and tall pine trees. Mimi's grave wasn't the open pit I had imagined.

My father recalls me tugging at his side and saying, "I'm glad I got to go to the cemetery today. It's a pretty place. I'm glad they're not going to put Mimi in just some hole in the ground."

According to my father's recollection, I understood a grave to be like any other hole in the ground. A pit. A gully. A crater. Even a trash dump. In my limited five-year-old life experience, I honestly thought that Mimi was going to be thrown in some type of open pit or trash dump. When I discovered the cemetery was nothing like I thought it would be, my fears were met with open relief.

It's a Matter of Truth

As a funeral director, my father has met with thousands of families going through the difficult process of burying a loved one. In those years, he has seen parents, grandparents, aunts, uncles, and family friends say just about everything imaginable to their children about death and dying. In many cases, the truth of what was really said to children was more about lying than dying. In other cases, adults simply communicated in language too complicated or too confusing for children to understand. My father has seen too many people unprepared to talk to their children about death, dying, and eternal life.

If you were a child unfamiliar with the ideas and concepts associated with death and dying, what kinds of thoughts would be developing in your mind if an adult told you . . .

"Grandpa went 'to sleep.'"
"Your baby sister went away."
"God needed another angel in heaven."
"Grandma went away on a long trip."
"Your father is 'resting in peace.'"
"Your mother passed on to another life."
"The good die young."

Children accept things for what they are. They need not be lied to. After all, it was a child who was willing to tell the truth about the emperor's new clothes.

Some adults may be afraid or unwilling to talk with children about death and dying because they are confused about their own spiritual beliefs.

I do not believe that the majority of parents actually intend to lie to their children. It is the rare pathological parents who lie to their children with the motivation of inflicting severe emotional harm. What is more common are parents and family members who are not in touch with their own feelings and beliefs about death and dying. This state of uncertainty leaves adults very ill equipped to speak with children.

There may be unresolved grief from the past. The memory of a parent, sibling, or friend who died years earlier may still haunt the person who has not worked through his feelings about death and the loss he experienced. There may be unresolved guilt. Anger. Confusion. Suppressed thoughts, feelings, and memories. All of these inner emotional conflicts make it very difficult for a person to speak with children or to anyone else about such a painful subject.

Some adults may be afraid or unwilling to talk with children about death and dying because they are confused about their own spiritual beliefs. They reason, "How can I talk about God and heaven when I'm not even sure what I believe?" Other adults might be angry at God or have all sorts of questions about who God is. Perhaps they were told as a child that it was God's will that a loved one died; right then and there, they refused to ever have anything to do with him again.

Perhaps the most common explanation for parents or family members who are unwilling to explore questions of death, dying, and eternal life with their children is that they are simply afraid to die. A conversation about death, even when no one has recently died, strikes an uncomfortable twinge of fear in the heart and raises all sorts of uncomfortable questions about eternal destinations.

When a death does strike a family, the natural and immediate reaction is shock and confusion. For adults who have not explored their own deep feelings about death and eternity, how can they possibly know what to say to a child? In a crisis situation like this, the most common reaction of adults is to communicate with children using trite sayings, euphemisms, and stock religious phrases. In the worst scenarios, a child is told absolutely nothing and expected to behave like a good little boy or girl as if nothing was wrong. What usually occurs is that a child is simply told incorrect or incomplete information about the events surrounding the death.

This is where we can do better.
This is where we must do better.

By truthfully communicating the news of a death in a simple way our children can understand, we invite them to participate in the loss the whole family is experiencing. Our goal is not to shelter or remove our children from a painful situation, but to communicate the correct information in such a way that they can enter the grieving process in a healthy manner. If a parent or relative died a very painful death, we do not have to mislead our children by saying this person felt no pain when he or she died. Though it is not necessary to give excessive detail, if a child asks whether or not the person died a painful death, it is perfectly acceptable to say, "Yes, your uncle was in a lot of pain when he died." It is also helpful to tell a child the context in which the illness occurred and how the fatal illness is unique from other common illnesses: "Uncle Rob had a disease called leukemia. His disease was very different than having a cold or an upset stomach."

By being truthful with our children, we are preparing them for the future times in their lives when they will revisit the ever-present reality of life and death. Our goal is to help our children understand their feelings and emotions within the grieving process. At the same time, we want to give them our comfort and loving reassurance by demonstrating a faith that endures in good times and in hard times. If we are going to be truthful to God, our children, and ourselves, one of the most significant ways to model the hope of heaven is by honestly communicating the painful realities of earth.

As parents and role models to our children, we can learn to communicate about life and death in simple and direct ways. Particularly in cases of murder, suicide, or grisly accidents, it is not necessary to give all of the explicit and graphic details. Depending on the age and emotional makeup of the child, this can be especially harmful. However, when a death does occur, we can talk about who died, what caused the death, what will happen at the funeral, what specific terms and unfamiliar concepts mean, what the Bible says about life and death, and what emotions the child can expect to feel. Taking the time to answer the dozens of questions our children will ask in the weeks, months, and yes, even years to come will have lasting effects. By refusing to give pat answers, avoid their questions, shade the truth, or resort to blatant lies, we will avoid sentencing our children to years of unlearning the lies they innocently believed. In confronting the harsh reality of death, we would do well to practice what we often tell our children: Tell the truth. There is simply no better way to earn their trust.

It's a Matter of Trust

Suffering with brain cancer, Charlotte Dean experienced periodic seizures while at home with her husband and two children. Knowing her illness was having a powerful effect on their two children, her husband, Todd, took action to help the whole family deal with the situation.

Todd had a specific plan for making sure Josh (five years old) and Sarah (three years old) knew what was going on. If Charlotte had a seizure at night, Josh and Sarah knew ahead of time they would be going next door to spend the night at Ed and Mary's while Daddy was at the hospital.

Before the kids went next door, Todd made sure they both saw the ambulance in front of the house. He also made sure they saw their mommy loaded into the ambulance and driven away. He always wanted the kids to know exactly what had happened to their mom and where she had gone. Todd always promised his kids he'd be home in the morning; even after being up all night at the hospital, he'd make sure he was home just as he had promised. The issue of trust was critical. He didn't want Josh or Sarah to ever feel as if they couldn't trust him.

Todd's actions illustrate the critical relationship between truth and trust. His deliberate and intentional steps to keep his children informed about what was happening to their mother during a crisis situation is an excellent example of honoring the holy gift of a child's trust. Todd's thoughtful preparation provided direction, comfort, and the reassurance Sarah and Josh needed during the prolonged period of Charlotte's illness.

> *Telling children the truth of what happens when a loved one dies is intricately connected to the whole of their life and faith.*

Kids live and breathe on their parents' every word. Kids put their confidence in what their parents communicate to them. They instinctively trust everything their parents say. Telling children the truth of what happens when a loved one dies is intricately connected to the whole of their life and faith. Trust is the essential element in all human relationships; nowhere is the foundation for the development of trust more influential than in the relationship between a parent and a child. The trust of a child is trust in its most sacred form.

Even Jesus often marveled at the faith and trust of little children. Knowing that children instinctively trust adults, Jesus issued some of his strongest words against those who might cause children to stumble: "But if anyone causes one of these little ones who believe in me to sin, it would be better for him to have a large millstone hung around his neck and to be drowned in the depths of the sea" (Matt. 18:6).

It's a Matter of Time

Perhaps you have small children and you've found it very difficult to communicate even the simplest concepts about death and dying to them. Maybe your children are more interested in watching Disney videos than talking about a dying relative. Or maybe it's been months since a death in your family occurred and you still haven't gotten a single word out of your son or daughter. Not only is teaching your child about death, dying, and eternal life a matter of truth and a matter of trust, it is also a matter of time. The biggest challenge you may face is simply making the time. Maybe you've been waiting and looking for the right time, the right words.

As we talk about truth, trust, and timing, it's important to remember that you can't force your children to talk about something that makes them feel uncomfortable. Given a safe environment and someone they can trust, kids will speak when they are ready. Just because a child is silent about his feelings does not mean he isn't thinking about the person who died. Unfortunately, it is usually the crying child who gets the most attention and comfort at a funeral; the silent child is often overlooked. Don't misinterpret silence as indifference. There is no one right way for your children to grieve. Talking with your children may simply be a matter of time.

You may have an eight-year-old who openly cries at the kitchen table over the loss of her favorite grandparent while your three-year-old happily dumps his Cheerios on the tile floor. As your children grow older, so will their understanding of life and death. Don't be discouraged if your best efforts to talk with your children are met with disinterest. Life presents plenty of opportunities to talk about important matters with our children. Given the opportunity and a safe environment, children will share their feelings when they are ready.

It sometimes takes gentle prodding with a leading question or a creative story to get your kids talking. Or perhaps your kids will blurt out a spontaneous question while driving home in the car or while sitting at the dinner table. They may ask tough questions at what seem to be inappropriate times. Right time . . . wrong time. Talking with your children isn't so much a matter of readiness as it is willingness. No matter how or when the subject comes up, it is important that you take the time to talk with your children about their thoughts and feelings concerning life and death. You will be making an essential investment in their spiritual and emotional development.

Put a Label on It

Call it what it is. Death is death, and if kids are going to be able to talk to their friends about what happened to their father, mother, brother, sister, friend, or relative, they need to label death for what it is. A label is a specific description of the origin and cause of death. "Sickness" is not a label—"lymphoma cancer" is. "An accident" is not a label—"a car accident caused by a drunk driver" is. "Went home to be with the Lord" is not a label—"a heart attack" is.

When children are given inadequate labels for death or told white lies, half-truths, or garbled religious gobbledygook, not only can they become confused, their social interactions can become difficult. Yes, it may be theologically correct for a six-year-old boy to say, "My dad went home to be with the Lord," but is that what a kid is really supposed to say to his friends when they ask why his dad didn't show up for T-ball practice? A simpler explanation is, "My dad died of a heart attack." Of course, a young child can express his confidence that his dad is in heaven, but it is essential for children to be able to communicate a clear, specific explanation of a death.

All children have a right to know how a loved one died. They need to know that death is not associated with every accident or illness. Depending on their age, children may not be able to separate how death is different from sickness and how accidents vary in degree of severity. Children need to know that there is a significant difference between an illness and a fatal illness. They need to know the distinction between a fender-bender car accident and a fatal car accident. They need to know that not all cancer is terminal. They need to know that everyone who goes to a hospital does not die. Why is this so important? A child's traumatic loss of a loved one is closely related to the immediate fear of losing someone else. To simply say that Grandma died because she was sick raises the question in a child's mind, "Will my mommy also die if she becomes sick? Will I die if I get sick?"

Becky Pines explained to her son, Josh, that his father did not just die while skiing, but died in a ski accident caused by an avalanche. As adults, we know there is a very significant difference between a simple ski accident and an avalanche. But, if all Josh was ever told was that his dad died while skiing, what kinds of assumptions about skiing would he assimilate in his mind?

Even if Josh doesn't know what an avalanche is now, he will eventually learn what one is. At that point in time, whether he's watching the Discovery Channel or reading a magazine article about natural wonders, Josh will discover what an avalanche is. He will make the connection that it was an avalanche and not simply a ski accident that killed his father. He will not have to unlearn or relearn what he has been told. The truth of what he has been told by his mother will be confirmed by his experience.

Damaging Spiritual Sound Bites

Let's face one simple fact: The trouble with talking to kids about heaven is that all of us are still here on earth. Our knowledge of heaven is limited. For all of the mile-long beaches and vast deserts on this planet, our understanding of the Almighty is about as big as a single grain of sand. Though the Bible is clear about the reality and the promise of heaven, the story is not yet in on the nature of God's eternal kingdom.

Because we have such a limited understanding of heaven and are often unsure what to say to children when a death occurs, we may be tempted to sidestep truth and real matters of faith in favor of "spiritually correct" answers or spiritual sound bites. We can fall into the trap of offering little more than vague theological assumptions and incorrect explanations in discussing eternal matters with our children. In a desperate effort to minimize the pain and tragedy of a difficult situation, we unwittingly become religious spin doctors. Unfortunately, the spin we give children can leave them confused and bewildered about the authentic nature and character of God as revealed in Scripture. Let's look at a few examples of damaging spiritual sound bites adults say to children (and other adults) without considering the full implications of their words.

Home with the Lord

"Your mother is home with the Lord; she's in a better place now." Most children, even most adults, have a hard time conceptualizing where heaven is and what it is like. The Bible gives us a quick sketch of heaven, particularly in the Book of Revelation, but I have a sneaking suspicion that our understanding of heaven is about as limited as a two-year-old's understanding of the need to share. Comprehending the reality of an unseen heaven as well as an unseen Lord is extremely difficult for a child. From a developmental viewpoint, the ability to discern abstract concepts comes only later in life; even then, these are concepts no child or adult can ever fully understand.

What most children do understand is the concept of home life. The home is the center of a child's world. To tell a child that his or her parent is in a better place now simply begs a series of troubling questions: *What was wrong with our home? Didn't Mommy like it here? Why would she want to go to a better place? Was I bad? Did I do something to make Mommy want to go away? Didn't Daddy love us enough to want to stay at our home? Why did God take Daddy from my home to his home?*

Can you see where these probing questions are leading? How can Jesus' Dad, the heavenly Father children learn and sing about in Sunday school, be the same God who steals a loved one away to a better place called heaven? In a child's eyes, this God is selfish. He is mean. He makes *The Grinch Who Stole Christmas* look like the Easter Bunny. He is the same cold, capricious, unloving God that countless numbers of adults rejected as children when they were told the lie that God took their mommy or daddy away to a better place. This is not the God of the Bible.

If a child perceives in any way that a choice was involved—either on the part of God or the loved one who died—to leave home in order to be in a "better place," then the deep fear of abandonment is realized in the life of that child. Not only does the child have to deal with the loss of a parent or sibling, he must also deal with abandonment issues that can cause severe emotional and spiritual harm.

Yes, heaven is a better place than earth. Yes, heaven is our true home. Yes, our loved ones who have died in Christ are no longer suffering like they did here on earth. But what we teach children about God and heaven needs to be separated from their understanding of home and their relationship to the person who died.

It doesn't help a child to compare their home to God's home. Who could compete with that? The last thing we want to do is alienate a child from God and the person who died. We must offer reassurance that the person who died didn't choose to leave the child. We can explain what the Bible does say about heaven in order to provide hope. In cases of suicide, we can explain to the child that the person who died was in deep emotional pain and the only way he saw to end the pain was to take his own life.[2] But again, in everything we say to a child, we would do best to eliminate spiritual sound bites. Instead, we can first try to understand a child's perception of our words and, when appropriate, offer simple words of comfort and reassurance.

The Lord's Will

"It was the Lord's will." This is a biggie. In the many interviews and research I conducted for this book, I learned this is the one phrase that bothers grieving people the most. Both sincere Christians and people who do not profess faith in Christ have trouble with this spiritual sound bite, especially when coupled with other nice-sounding phrases like, "It was a blessing," and, "God will never give you more than you can handle, blah . . . blah . . . blah." The profound loss a grieving person is experiencing is minimized by such insensitive and sappy spiritual babbling. If a grieving person finds peace in accepting the death of a loved one as the will of God—fine. This type of grace is a gift from God; but for grieving people, it is a grace that is usually received only after long periods of painful searching and sleepless nights. Accepting the death of a loved one usually happens *on the other side* of the valley of the shadow of death. Acceptance is rarely found *in* the valley, and that is what makes it so difficult to hear someone chirp, "It must have been the Lord's will."

How can we be so flippant? Why must we minimize other people's pain with such spiritual drivel? What kinds of messages are we branding on kids' hearts in the name of God? Why do we feel we have to speak for God when God himself chooses, at times, to remain silent?

By telling a grieving person it was God's will their loved one died, we are writing an insensitive and ineffective prescription for their pain.

Telling a grieving child or adult it was the Lord's will that their loved one died not only shows insensitivity to that person's relationship with God, it also trivializes the name of God to the point of contempt. There is no greater, more powerful force on earth to crush a person's spirit than the power of death. How much worse can it be living with the knowledge that the God of the universe has inflicted the tremendous burden of death on a human being? From a biblical perspective, death is *not* the will of God but the result of humanity's rebellion against God. By telling a grieving person that it was God's will that their loved one died, we are writing an insensitive and ineffective prescription for their pain.

The phrase "God's will" only appears a few times throughout the entire Bible. When used, it usually refers to our character, our choices, and our conduct as followers of Christ and *not* to the mind of God. The Bible asks over and over, "Who can know the mind of God?" In the Old Testament, God spoke through the prophet Isaiah when he said, "'For my thoughts are not your thoughts, neither are your ways my ways,' declares the LORD. 'As the heavens are higher than the earth, so are my ways higher than your ways and my thoughts than your thoughts'" (Isa. 55:8–9). And in the New Testament, the apostle Paul wrote, "Oh, the depth of the riches of the wisdom and knowledge of God! How unsearchable his judgments, and his paths beyond tracing out! 'Who has known the mind of the Lord? Or who has been his counselor?'" (Rom. 11:33–34).

Both Isaiah and Paul belong to a select group of people in the Bible who actually stood in the presence of God. If they themselves said very few words about the will of God, it would be better for us to not presume to know the Lord's will for someone else.

God Needed an Angel

"God needed another angel." Ask any parent whose child has died if the explanation that "God needed another angel" provided an adequate sense of comfort for their traumatic loss. The odds are ten to one you'll hear the following response: "God has millions of angels . . . why did he take *my* angel?"

For many grieving people, the angel thing just doesn't cut it. For people of faith—and even for those who make no claim to faith—this spiritual sound bite begs the following questions: "God has everything. Why would he need another angel? If God is truly the Creator, why would he destroy a life when he can create anything he wants or needs?"

Why do so many of us buy the angel shtick? Why do we tell hurting people that their deceased loved ones are now angels? The first and most obvious reason is that as kids, most of us fantasized about how great it would be to have wings like an angel so we could cruise through the clouds. Who wouldn't like to fly like an angel?

Second, angels are adorable. Not only are Raphael's chubby little cherubs popularized on T-shirts, greeting cards, key chains, and picture frames, angels also receive plenty of popular attention in movies, TV shows, and magazines.

Third, angels are closer to God than any living being on earth. What could be a higher calling than to be a personal assistant to the most high God? Angels are God's servants. They are protectors. Guardians. Messengers. Worshipers. Ministers of the Almighty. Everything angels do is in direct response to their intimate relationship with God. Angels share a closeness with God that represents our deepest longings for perfection and intimacy with our Creator.

Last, it would be completely un-American if Jimmy Stewart's encounter with Clarence, the angel in *It's a Wonderful Life,* was not one of our favorite movie scenes. Who are we to keep an angel from earning his wings?

But there is a lot of honest confusion about angels today. In teaching children about heaven, adults must be clear on what the Bible says about angels. There are many sincere people who believe that when they die, they will become angels. From a biblical perspective, this simply isn't true. The angel worship so prevalent in our society today, especially in popular New Age best-sellers, offers a thin, but misleading veneer of hope.

As servants of almighty God, angels have an important place in God's kingdom, but the Bible is very clear that angels do not have to earn their wings. And human beings do not become angels any more than babies become chubby little cherubs in bas-relief. Angels are servants of God, and any time an angelic encounter is recorded in Scripture, the angel's main purpose is to direct a person's attention toward the God of the Old and New Testaments. Angels are *never* to be worshiped. They are never to be sought for spiritual direction (see Rev. 22:8–9). So strong is this sentiment in Scripture that the apostle Paul wrote, "Evidently some people are throwing you into confusion and are trying to pervert the gospel of Christ. But even if we or an angel from heaven should preach a gospel other than the one we preached to you, let him be eternally condemned!" (Gal. 1:7–8).

Strong words. Yet there are still many individuals with good intentions who pass on the modern-day myth to grieving people that "God needed another angel."

Making an Honest Start

Depending on their ages, your children may not be able to grasp abstract concepts such as *forever, eternity, heaven,* and yes, even *death*. However, don't allow what *you think* your children can't understand to discourage you from speaking with them.

Oh yeah, and don't worry about flubbing what you say. Tripping over your words for the sake of truth is far more valuable than eloquence laced with errors. You are beginning a discussion with your children that you will revisit again and again over the course of their lifetime. What your children do not grasp now, they will understand later. (Or maybe they are the ones who've got this faith thing figured out and they're not letting us in on their secrets!)

Your truthfulness will help develop a lasting sense of security in your children's lives. Your sensitivity to their feelings and their need to grieve will tell them how important they are to you. Your honesty will provide a snapshot of integrity that they can keep in the wallet of their hearts for the rest of their lives.

Your truthfulness will let your children know that it's okay to cry.

5

It's Okay to Cry

Good Grief for Children

> Crying is a means by which you work your way out of the depths of despair. Of course your weeping will not bring your loved one back. But that's why you cry. Because you cannot bring your beloved back to life.
>
> Earl A. Grollman

Josh Pines was four years old when his mother, Becky, took him to visit his father's grave for the first time. Josh was only three months old when his father, Tim Pines, left in the early morning hours with a buddy, Charlie Prior, to go skiing at Mount Baldy, a Southern California ski area known for its steep, rugged terrain. The night before, an unusually strong winter snowstorm moved into Southern California, depositing record amounts of powdery snow like a thick, heavy blanket across the rumpled San Bernardino Mountains. Mount Baldy would be steep and deep with fresh powder— a skier's dream. Both Tim and Charlie were expert skiers as well as thoughtful husbands who knew the value of making a phone call if they were going to be late.

When Tim didn't arrive home at his estimated 5:00 P.M. arrival time, Becky didn't think much of it. She had just finished watching the news, which had reports of heavy traffic on the 405 freeway due to the heavy rain. Tim was usually good about calling, but he was probably stuck in traffic, so Becky figured he was having a hard time getting to a phone.

At 7:30 P.M., Becky called Charlie's wife, Ellen, to ask if she had heard from Charlie. Ellen told Becky that Charlie hadn't called yet. Naturally, both women began to wonder if something had happened to their husbands.

By midnight, there was still no word from Tim or Charlie. Becky placed a call to Paul Pines, Tim's brother who works for the highway patrol. She asked Paul if any accidents had been reported involving Tim or Charlie, or if it was possible to find out if their car was still in the parking lot at Mount Baldy. Paul promised to help try to locate his missing brother and told Becky he would call her back as soon as possible.

Becky's telephone rang at 2:00 A.M. with news from Paul that Tim and Charlie's car had been found in the Mount Baldy parking lot. The most logical conclusion to the mystery of their disappearance was that Tim and Charlie were still somewhere up on the mountain. Immediate plans were made for a search-and-rescue team to be sent out at dawn. Friends and family were called and dozens of friends arrived at the ski area the next day to help in the rescue efforts.

As heavy snow, thick clouds, and twisting fog swirled through the trees around Mount Baldy in near whiteout conditions, over one hundred volunteers and professional rescue workers began the search for Tim and Charlie on the precipitous, avalanche-prone slopes. While friends and family covered the terrain on and near the slopes, the professional search-and-rescue team went into the backcountry to see if Tim and Charlie had ventured into the extremely dangerous, out-of-bounds territory of Coldwater Canyon.

The first day's rescue efforts yielded nothing and no one. Not a single ski glove or ski pole. No track marks. No goggles. Not a trace of Tim or Charlie. Thus began a three-month-long search by numerous rescue teams, government agencies (with phone calls to the FBI), and friends and family who scoured the mountain in search of these two men. The prevailing opinion was that Tim and Charlie had most likely been killed in an avalanche. Despite discouragement and frustration from no progress being made in the rescue efforts, Becky refused to believe that Tim was dead until the discovery of his body proved otherwise.

On Sunday, May 3, three of Becky's friends were once again searching the slopes of Coldwater Canyon when they discovered a pair of goggles. As their search continued, they came upon another item—a ski pole sticking out of the melting snow. Finally, as the threesome examined the surrounding area, they discovered a partially uncovered piece of material that matched the description of Charlie Prior's ski suit. After hanging on to a slim thread of hope for three months that both men, against all odds, might somehow still be alive, Becky was hit all at once with the harsh realization that both men were dead.

Six days later, on Becky's birthday, search-and-rescue volunteers finally discovered Tim's body near the site where Charlie had been found. Becky's worst fears were confirmed: Tim and Charlie had been swept down the side of Mount Baldy in an avalanche. According to the autopsy report, both men had been killed instantly; their bodies were entombed in approximately eighty feet of snow and ice.

Four years later, as the cold February rain drizzled down from the gray skies above, Becky and Josh stopped at a florist to buy some flowers to place on Tim's grave. It was Tim's birthday, February 20, 1996, and since Josh was now four years old, Becky knew it was time to help him understand a little bit more about his father. So far, the memory of Tim had been kept alive through family photos, videotapes, and the stories shared by family and friends.

Arriving at Pacific View Cemetery, which overlooks the ocean and the boat-filled harbor of Newport Beach, Becky and Josh hopped out of the car and walked on the gentle, green slopes toward Tim's grave. Flowers in hand, Becky showed Josh where his father was buried. After spending a short time talking about his dad and asking questions about the cemetery, Josh looked up at Becky and said, "I really miss my daddy. Maybe the raindrops will wash my tears away?"

Getting Lost in "the Loss"

When children lose a parent, grandparent, sibling, relative, or a pet, they experience a profound sense of loss just as adults do. Grief is not age specific. A death is a death and a loss is a loss. Death has a tremendous impact on everyone. However, it has been said that when a death occurs, children are often the *silent mourners*. In the frenzy of making funeral arrangements, having family and guests at the house, planning for a memorial service and reception, taking and making phone calls, speaking with doctors, police officers, lawyers, business partners, and dealing with dozens of other details, let alone trying to deal with the personal shock of what has just happened, it is easy for children to get lost in "the loss." Adults are literally speaking over the heads of children using words and concepts unfamiliar to them.

When a death occurs, children are often the silent mourners.

Every grieving experience is unique. Just as adults grieve in different ways, so do children. Depending on the age and life experience of the children, perceptual and developmental differences in their understanding of death will have an impact on how they view the loss of the loved one. Much research has been completed in child and adolescent bereavement that can greatly aid us in understanding how to best help children and teenagers cope with the loss of a loved one. Before exploring a number of helpful ways to prevent your child from getting lost in "the loss," let's look at a child's understanding of death from a developmental perspective.

How Children Understand Death

A lot of good and helpful material has been written about child and adolescent bereavement, but the majority of it comes from a perspective that does not attempt to integrate issues of faith and spirituality. Our challenge is to understand how children view death with the goal of helping them in their faith development. In order to prepare our children for this life and eternal life, we need to find practical ways of integrating concepts of faith with a child's understanding of death. While this sounds like a daunting task, somewhere in the middle of explaining the Trinity, what a soul looks like, and why Lucky Charms have that chalky taste, a few guiding principles will help you in this important lifelong process:

Make a commitment to talk to your children about life and death in simple words and concepts they can understand.

Help your children to understand, identify, and act on their emotions in healthy ways.

Continue to talk to your children about life and death as they grow and develop.

Raise your children, as best you can, with the solid hope of heaven.

Don't allow your fear of not having "all" of the answers or the "right" answers to keep you from giving your children "some" of the answers about life and death.

Children's understanding of death depends on their age, cognitive development, life experience, and the amount of information they have received. As they go from being infants to toddlers to young children and on into adolescence, they grow in their understanding of life and death. They go from seeing death as something temporary and reversible to comprehending that all people will eventually die. They move from viewing death as an insidious villain like the Grim Reaper to realizing that death has strong and lasting consequences.

An infant has no cognitive understanding of death. However, an infant can sense loss by the absence of its primary nurturer, which in most cases is the mother. In the case of Josh, who was only three months old when his father died, death was experienced (if not understood) as the absence of the bonding relationship he had shared with his father. An infant is dependent on others for its survival, comfort, nurture, and growth. Since infants and very small children do not have a concept of time, death is experienced as the void or absence of someone who was previously close to the child.

Preschoolers and toddlers understand death to be a temporary, reversible, and impersonal event. Think about the cartoon characters they watch on TV: Wile E. Coyote has been blown up, smashed, poisoned, launched, impaled, and squished into an accordion a zillion times over, yet he still lives. That little "poof" of dust at the bottom of the gaping, thousand-foot cliff must be the exhale of the airbag he lands on every time.

Cartoon characters who come back to life again and again reinforce the notion that death is something temporary, almost funny, for young children. Since death is not understood as something permanent, when a family member or a pet dies, preschoolers may continue to talk about them as if they hadn't died. A toddler may constantly ask when Mommy or Daddy is coming home or when the pet hamster is going to wake up.

Some time between the ages of five and nine, children begin to understand that death is permanent and lasting, but it is still seen as an impersonal force. They don't believe death is something that will happen to them. In one way or another, they think they can trick death or escape from death by their own ingenuity. During this developmental stage, children often understand death to be the boogeyman, the angel of death, the Grim Reaper, a ghost, goblin, or other evil force that kills people. Death is understood to be something external or something that happens only because of an outside factor. These children have not completely grasped the fact that not only does everyone die, but they, too, will also someday die.

It is during this stage that children take death very seriously in the elaborate rituals and ceremonies they perform. Take a pet funeral for example: When a pet dies, children carefully plan and perform graveside services for the dead animal. Prayers are said. Simple eulogies are given. The animal is buried with his tags, feeding bowl, leash, or some other kind of special memento. A tombstone or solitary cross marks the spot where the animal lies. Though children may not view death as something personal that will happen to them, they understand death as a permanent reality.

In the years of preadolescence, children between the ages of ten and twelve now understand death as a permanent, irreversible reality that not only affects others, but themselves as well. At this stage, preteens know that every living thing dies. They know that they will die. They begin to ponder and consider abstract concepts such as eternity, spirituality, heaven, and hell. Comic books, video games, movies, and videos with strong death themes are very popular among this age group. Preteens, like older teenagers, are fascinated and influenced by the violent movies in theaters today. Many of these movies have strong spiritual themes dealing with heaven and hell, angels, reincarnation, satanic forces, witchcraft, spiritism, demons, and life after death. Some of these movies may contain a few kernels of spiritual truth, but hardly enough to fill a tub of popcorn, let alone provide a satisfying and lasting spiritual hope for the future. Though a child may be raised in a Christian home, he or she can easily be influenced by the spiritual messages in these movies.

When a child grows into adolescence, death is viewed clearly as permanent, certain, and unchanging. What is changing, though, is the teenager. From sexual and physical changes, to the power of peer influence, to new responsibilities at home, school, and work, a teenager is in the powerful throes of change. As a teenager grows and encounters new life experiences, so does his or her understanding of death.

It is almost impossible today for a young person to attend high school for four years and not experience the death of a friend or acquaintance at school. Since automobile accidents, alcohol and drug abuse, and suicide are common causes of death among teenagers, and since these topics receive a substantial amount of media attention, teenagers have a heightened awareness of death. Heavy metal, gangsta rap, grunge, and alternative rock music carry heavy themes of death, desperation, depression, and dysfunction. World events such as starvation, wars, terrorist attacks, and other natural disasters are also seen daily on television.

Teenagers are curious about death and are interested in exploring abstract questions of eternity and the afterlife. Many teenagers are afraid of death, and they will go to great lengths to overcome their fear of death by drag racing, performing dangerous stunts, or engaging in other death-defying maneuvers. Some teenagers are reckless because

It's Okay to Cry

they think they will never die; they think they are invincible. As crazy as it sounds, many teenagers live as if they were cats with nine lives. Chapter 9 is designed to help parents and other adults understand, communicate, and help teenagers who've lost a loved one.

Your Child's Emotions

God has given children a colorful and powerful palette of emotions. Never are those emotions put to the test more than when a loved one dies. Just as every child has a unique personality, every child will respond to loss in a different way. The wide range of emotions children experience as they mourn can be seen in their actions and their attitudes. If your child or the child of someone you know has recently experienced the death of a loved one, here are some emotions you may see.

Anger

Justin, age eight, said, "I want to slug God because he took my baby away. And when I see my brother in heaven, I'm going to have to pound him. Then I'll hug him, 'cause I've missed him so much." Anger is a common reaction to loss among children. When events and circumstances happen that are out of a child's control, anger is a way of expressing profound displeasure and emotional discomfort. Anger is a clear sign that a child is hurting inside. As in Justin's case, children may be angry at the baby who died. They may be angry at God because someone told them that God needed another angel. They may be angry at their parents for ignoring their need for information on what has happened as well as their need for love, attention, and comfort. From a deep-seated sense of self-preservation, children may even be angry out of fear that they may be the next to die.

Anger serves to protect the inner world of children, which has been attacked by the loss of someone they loved. Anger is a self-defense mechanism that strikes at the injustice of death. It is born out of a need for security and protection. For children, anger is an appropriate response to the chaos that has entered their world and violated their sense of well-being. Anger serves as a critical internal warning light that furiously flashes inside children when they believe their life is in danger. What could be more dangerous to the heart, mind, and spirit of a child than the loss of a loved one? What could be more frightening than the experience of grief?

Just as every child has a unique personality, every child will respond to loss in a different way.

Though anger is a God-given emotion, many children are raised with the notion that anger is bad. Not only is anger bad, some children are told, it is also wrong and sinful. Children are warned that if they become angry at God, then God will become angry with them.

In the Bible, particularly in the Old Testament, we often see an angry God. But what is he angry about? He is angry at injustice, sin, the wicked treatment of widows and orphans, hypocritical religious practices, oppression, hard hearts, and tyranny. If we see anger displayed in the character of God and we know that anger is a human emotion, why do we teach children that anger is wrong?

Paul tells us in Ephesians 4:26, "In your anger do not sin." However, Paul does not say anger is sinful. When he saw his Father's temple turned into a fraudulent animal house, Jesus whipped up a hefty serving of good ol' righteous anger. Jesus taught us how to get angry about the right things.

78

Anger is a passionate response to injustice. For some children who feel angry at the loss of a loved one, anger can be just what they need to vent their sense of injustice. We do not have to be afraid of allowing our children to become angry. Rather, we can help our children deal with anger in healthy, constructive ways.

Better for a child to pound a pillow than to pound a little sister.

Better to go to the batting cage than to live with rage swinging inside.

Better to go walking with someone who will listen than to brood in silence.

Better to find a creative outlet like drawing, dancing, or painting than for a child's fragile sense of self to be crushed by the oppression of unreleased anger.

Nobody knows your children better than you . . . what is their outlet for anger? If we teach our children that anger is wrong, unacceptable, or sinful, we will be cutting off the necessary process of grief. Not allowing children to express their anger can lead to emotional suffocation. Stuffed anger is usually vented through negative, destructive behavior. If anger is not released, then it will eventually surface later in life much to the harm of all.

Guilt

Another common emotion children feel after the death of a loved one is guilt. For varying reasons, children may think that it is their fault the person died. Particularly with accidents, children can feel that they in some way caused the accident or that they could have prevented the accident.

Children also feel guilty when they are helpless in comforting their inconsolable parents. Since death has a tremendous impact on the landscape of family life, the guilty feelings children experience are often related to not knowing how to respond to the various needs of family members. Unknowingly, grieving parents can look to surviving children for a sense of comfort and support. Guilt is felt when a child cannot meet the needs and expectations of grieving family members, whether the perceived needs are real or not.

In her excellent book *Beyond Grief*, Carol Staudacher describes various self-punishing thoughts and guilty feelings children may experience, particularly after the death of a sibling. Some of their thoughts might be:

Last week he wanted to borrow my baseball mitt and I didn't loan it to him.

My sister interrupted my phone call and I screamed at her.

The baby cried and I was busy talking to my friends in the driveway so I didn't tell my mother. She was just next door.

He got a D in math and I . . . made fun of him because all my grades were high. I called him "stupid."

After my sister was born, I was really jealous. I wanted things to be the way they were before her birth.[3]

Children can feel guilty after a death for all sorts of reasons. It is the wise adult who can help a young person sort out the difference between real guilt (i.e., remorse over doing something wrong) and false guilt.

Sadness

When a child is told in a clear and honest way that someone has died, the natural emotional response is sadness. Dealing with loss—any type of loss—produces sadness in children and adults alike. Children need to know it's okay to feel sad. Their sadness may be expressed in tears. They may walk around the house in what seems to be a perpetual pout. Silence and withdrawal can also be expressions of sadness. A sad child may want to be constantly held or hugged. Depending on a child's age, temperament, and personality, sadness may be seen in moodiness, irritability, or anxiety.

As children journey through the various emotions of grief in the weeks and months—yes, even years—after the death of a loved one, they need to understand that they will feel sadness from time to time. Their sadness needs to be validated as an appropriate response to the loss they've experienced. Occasionally, Josh Pines will openly express his sadness and longing for his father by telling Becky, "I really miss my daddy." When a child like Josh can freely share his feelings of sadness, he is grieving in a healthy manner. Sadness, like all the emotions related to grieving, needs a constant outlet. Without an outlet for intense emotions, a child will learn to build dangerous dams of denial. These dams, in one way or another, will eventually spring leaks and overflow in a torrential path of pain.

Fear

Death is a frightening concept for children. After the death of a loved one, it is critical for adults to take the fears of their children very seriously. Death sends intense shock waves of fear through a family, and it is easy for the smallest to get hit the hardest. Though every family member suffers in a deeply painful and personal way, children lack the life experience to completely understand what has happened. When left with inadequate information, lies, or silence, a child's mind can go ballistic with all sorts of fears, worries, doubts, and suspicions—both real and imagined. Throw in a few horrifying television images of the skull-faced Grim Reaper, flesh-devouring ghosts, and demonic characters clawing their way out of dirt-covered caskets, and a wicked batch of F-E-A-R is brewing in the heart of a very scared child.

As I mentioned earlier, children are often the silent mourners whose needs go unattended. Fear can send children running in all sorts of directions for the rest of their lives. Even though children—especially young children—may seem relatively unscathed by the death of a parent or sibling, fear is a dark current that can run deep inside their hearts, hidden from view. Chapter 6 is dedicated to exploring this sensitive issue in detail.

Confusion

Picture yourself as a child. A death has just occurred in your family. The only problem is that everyone knows about it except you.

The phone rang a couple days ago.

You, your parents, your brother and sister were having dinner.

It was someone calling about your older brother away at college.

Your mother crumpled to the kitchen floor in tears.

Your father grabbed the phone from her hand.

He finished the call and said good-bye.

People have been streaming in and out of the house ever since.

Your father looks grim. Numb. But people say he looks strong.

Your mother hasn't been out of bed much since that phone call.

You see your brother and sister and other people crying a lot.

None of this seems to make much sense.

Your house is filled with food and flowers.

Why is everyone so sad?

You hear strange words like *funeral, eulogy,* and *cremation.*
Your suitcase has been packed.
Nobody has said anything about a vacation.
You wish someone would tell you what's going on.
You wonder if you're going to visit your brother away at school.

Unless children are informed about what has happened when a death occurs, they are left to their own conclusions—correct or incorrect. Children become confused when a death occurs primarily because the routine of life around them has been turned upside-down. A death raises all sorts of questions in the mind of a child about safety, security, the future, changes in the family, and details surrounding the death itself: "What happened? Who died? How did they die? Am I going to die too? Who's going to take care of me now? Why do we have to sell our home? Why is everyone so sad? Why did Daddy have to die? Where is heaven? Why do I feel so bad inside? How come God let this happen?"

If the flurry of events and emotions within two to five days of a death are overwhelming for adults, imagine how difficult it is for a child to absorb what is going on. Some adults may feel that children don't truly understand what is happening when someone dies and that the impact of the death isn't as great on them. That may be true in some cases. For example, the death of a distant relative or a business associate the child rarely saw may not jolt the child's sense of security, especially if they still see Mom and Dad every day.

But in most cases, children become disoriented when a death occurs because they receive just enough limited information to make them confused. Children are smarter than most adults realize. They can make reasonable and correct conclusions even with limited information. At the same time, they can also make erroneous conclusions because of the surrounding confusion. If a caring adult has not clearly explained what has happened in simple words and phrases, children are left to sort out the bits and pieces of conversations they overhear and the observations they make of other family members. They must rely on a strong, intuitive sense that something bad has happened.

By understanding how death and the events surrounding a death can confuse children, parents can eliminate some of the emotional pain. Here are specific ways children become confused when a death occurs:

- The child has not been told a death has happened.
- The child is not told beforehand that someone critically ill may die.
- The child has been told someone has died, but in words they don't understand.
- The child knows someone has died, but isn't given accurate information.
- The child experiences waves of conflicting emotions.
- The child is not informed of important decisions.
- The child is told nothing is wrong and is expected to be a good little boy or girl.
- The child wonders why a loving God would allow a loved one to be taken away.
- The child is expected to give care and comfort to others.

Understanding how children grieve and how we communicate eternal truths to them has a major role in shaping their lives with an eternal perspective. We have the unique privilege of helping them honor and understand their God-given emotions.

The Benefits of Helping Children Grieve

When we help children grieve in healthy ways, we serve their best interests in a number of positive ways.

84

- We teach them how to label and understand their emotions.
- We show them that it's okay to feel pain, anger, fear, sorrow, and sadness.
- We prepare them with the knowledge that they will face numerous periods of grief over the course of their lives.
- We teach them critical life skills in knowing how to handle and deal with conflict.
- We model how to share feelings in an open and honest way.
- We earn their trust by not lying to them. Trust, a critical element to any healthy relationship, builds a sense of security in their lives.
- We help them to understand both positive and negative ways of handling emotions.
- We show them the importance of sharing compassion with those who are hurting.
- We teach them that their thoughts and feelings are important to us.
- We demonstrate a deep and sincere love for who they are today and the person they are growing up to be.

Helping your children handle their emotions just may give you a decent night's sleep. Well, maybe . . . it depends what kinds of monsters are in your closets.

6

Scared of the Dark

Dealing with Fear When Tragedy Strikes

Fear not, for I have redeemed you; I have summoned you by
name; you are mine. When you pass through the waters, I
will be with you; and when you pass through the rivers, they
will not sweep over you.

Isaiah 43:1–2

I remember clearly the night my oldest daughter, Janae,
snuggled into bed and told me how scared she was of her
family dying. She was four years old, and the memory of her
cousin, Matthew, who had died of SIDS eight months earlier was still very fresh in her mind.

We had just said our prayers when Janae looked up at me
with her big brown eyes full of tears.

"Daddy," she cried, "I don't want you to die."

What's prompting this? I thought. *Me, die? Who said anything about death?*

"That's okay, honey," I gently responded. "I know you don't
want me to die. I'm not planning on dying anytime soon.
Daddy's with you right now."

"No-o-o-o," she cried louder, "I don't want you to EVER die! I don't want you or Mommy or Ellie to EVER, EVER die. I just want to be with you and Mommy and Ellie forever."

Did I have a wonderful solution for my daughter? Magic words to calm her fears of losing her family? I guess a real Superdad could leap over jungle gyms in a single bound, stop a bullet with his teeth, and at the very least, overcome death. I wish I could say that I was that type of Superdad, but what I found that night was Janae did not want words; she simply wanted to be comforted. She wanted to be hugged and reassured that everything—even her fear-filled feelings—was okay. Though I couldn't take away her fears and I couldn't tell her I would never die, I could listen, comfort, and be sensitive to her feelings. Before we look at the fears a child may face when a loved one dies, let's first look at some of the other fears in a child's life.

There's Something in My Closet

When children and teenagers are scared, it's not uncommon for them to receive the following messages from their siblings, parents, and peers:

"Stop your whining and be a man."
"There is *nothing* to be afraid of."
"Big girls don't cry."
"Look . . . there is absolutely nothing in your closet."
"Stop being a scaredy-cat."
"Don't be a wuss."
"You're not chicken, are you?"
"Your friends never get scared like you do."
"Look at you! You're afraid of your own shadow."

As parents, we know our children experience both real and imagined fears. Walking down the street, we see our kids jump at the snapping bark of a passing poodle. That's a real fear. For "seat belt aware" children who've been admonished over and over about the dangers of riding in a car without one on, what parent hasn't heard the scream of panic, "Don't go yet—I haven't put my seat belt on!" Another real fear.

However, when it comes to putting the kids to bed (after the fifth glass of water and the twenty-eighth question), all of their imaginary fears come tumbling out of the closet like a horde of screaming banshees. There are goblins under the bed. Ghosts in the closet. Hideous monsters peeking in the window. Burglars waiting to break in. Sinister spirits in the shadows. I don't know about you, but if I ever find that "something" in my daughter's closet, I swear I'm gonna kill it!

As parents, we know that there is little chance of a monster exploding out of our children's closet. But we do have to convince them that the likelihood of their fear being realized is quite minimal. At times, our child's imaginary fears amount to blatant manipulation. The kid simply does not want to go to bed. We need to use wisdom to discern when our son or daughter is truly scared and when we're getting the sheets pulled over our eyes.

Our children, especially between the ages of three and five years old, go through various developmental stages such as being scared of the dark, playing with imaginary friends, and carrying a blanket. Understanding that these fears are part of their growing understanding of this world can help us help them put their fears in perspective. However, it is important to remember that when children are truly scared—when they sense a real and possible danger—the resulting fear produces all sorts of emotional reactions and questions.

Doubt. Fear causes doubt over the safety of loved ones.

Anxiety. Fear-produced worries cause feelings of insecurity and tension.

Suspicion. Fear creates uneasiness, not knowing who or what to trust.

Hesitation. Fear impedes good decision-making skills.

Anger. Fear can cause anger. Overt or repressed, anger often comes out in destructive ways.

Worthlessness. Fear can make children feel unloved, like nobody cares about them.

Loneliness. Fear can cause feelings of isolation and distance from others.

Guilt. Fear can make a child feel bad for feeling scared.

Hopelessness. Fear can cause overwhelming feelings of despair.

Depression. Fear often leads to depression. Numbed by feelings of emptiness, depression drains a child's spirit.

Let's be honest: We're all scared about something. We all get the heebie-jeebies. We're all chicken. Real or imagined, fear is a scary thing for a child afraid of that "something" in the closet or that monster under the bed. And when a loved one dies, a child's fear is particularly intense.

Fears a Child May Face When a Loved One Dies

What are the fears a child faces when a loved one dies? This is a question every parent needs to think about in terms of their child's unique personality and past experiences. When a relative or friend dies, the child must not only try to deal with the troublesome emotions of grief but also try to understand the many changes that are taking place in his or her family.

Though the world can be a scary place, all children really want is for their home to be the safest place on earth.

As everyone tries to cope with the death, the dynamics of family change can be unsettling for children. These changes, along with the death itself, can be the source of many fears. Family crises, whether short-lived or long-term, necessitate tremendous adjustments by each family member. Depending on how family members treat one another, what family members are permitted to talk about, and how the family responds to crises, these adjustments may greatly affect the children's capacity to understand, communicate, and cope with their fears. Though the world can be a scary place, all children really want is for their home to be the safest place on earth.

When a loved one dies, your child may experience any of the following fears.

Abandonment

There is nothing worse than a child's fear of being separated from or abandoned by his parents. The emotional and spiritual trauma of losing a parent, sibling, schoolmate, or relative can spark intense fears of being alone. Following a death, it's not uncommon for a child to fear being abandoned. A child may not want to leave her parents' side. The child may express fear of everyday events like going to school or to the grocery store. A child who previously played by himself alone with a room full of toys may not want to be left unattended. Physical symptoms, such as headaches, incontinence, and stomachaches, may surface at school because the child desires to be at home with Mom or Dad.

A death can make a child feel terribly lonely and isolated. Being left unattended, even for short periods of time, can ignite powerful feelings of anxiety and loss in a child who has been traumatized by the death of a loved one. The words, "Mommy! Daddy! Stay with me. Don't go!" are worth paying attention to; they signal a child in need of attention and reassurance.

Death

When children learn of a death, they fear that their death or the death of another loved one is imminent. Recognizing this fear, a child may wonder, *Am I going to die too? My grandpa died in his sleep. Will I die when I go to bed tonight?*

Depending on the cause of death, a child may associate death with a particular activity, place, or event. Death might be linked to a hospital, so the child develops a fear of hospitals. After a fatal car accident, a child may be afraid to ride in cars. Whatever causes the death can become a focus for the child's own fear of death. Pools. Playgrounds. Sickness and diseases. The child believes they will die in the same way. In the case of a deceased older sibling, the younger siblings may believe they, too, will die when they reach the age the older sibling was at the time of death.

Going to Sleep

Since sleep is a prolonged period of dark isolation from parents, brothers, and sisters, it's easy to see how going to bed can make a child feel scared and insecure. For many children, going to bed can be a terrifying experience even when no one has died. So when a death occurs, a child's normal fear of sleep can be escalated to greater levels. The terminology adults use to explain death to children doesn't help to alleviate the turmoil of this problem. Phrases such as "eternal slumber," "rest in peace," "eternal rest," and "Grandma has gone to sleep for a very long time," contribute to a child's equating sleep with death. What child would want to go to bed if they thought they wouldn't wake up for a very long time?

A child who is afraid to go to sleep may want to read book after book, may cry incessantly, or may take forever to get ready for bed. If your children keep hopping in your bed at night or asking you to sleep with them, their behavior (like so many things in the grief experience), could be related to their need for security. In many cases, wanting to sleep in the parents' bed lasts for a short season. However, if this becomes a prolonged battle and source of contention, you may want to seek professional help.

Nightmares are another common occurrence associated with the fear of going to sleep. The child may be terrified of a recurring nightmare. Going to sleep can conjure scary dreams reliving the accident, meeting the dead person, or confronting a horrible beast. Sleep disorders such as insomnia are a regular experience for children who lose a loved one. Find a local bereavement support group and ask for resources on children's sleep disorders. Understanding the dynamics of sleep disorders may help you help your children get the sleep they need. And you too!

Death of Parents and Other Loved Ones

For the majority of children, the home is the central source of security, protection, and well-being. The fear of losing one or both parents is a direct threat to a child's need for protection.

The story I told at the beginning of this chapter illustrates how powerful a child's fear of losing a parent or sibling can be. To deal with the intense fear of being alone, children may become clingy. They may whine and cry, never wanting to leave their parents' side. Business trips can become a source of anxiety for the child who is afraid of losing a parent to airplane, car, or train crashes.

To a child, a parent is everything. Instinctively, children look to parents for love, nurture, affirmation, protection, comfort, and physical provision. Even in abusive homes where only a child's basic needs for food, shelter, and warmth are met, the child may still experience the fear of a parent dying in some sort of tragic and unexpected way.

Showing Emotion

Whereas young children may openly cry and display emotions such as anger and sadness, older children may be afraid of showing emotion out of fear of saying or doing the wrong thing. An older child may feel guilty for making Mom cry. A brother or sister may get angry at a younger sibling for talking about the person who died.

Children may receive the implicit or explicit message that it is not okay to talk about a parent or sibling who has died. Grieving and open displays of emotion may not be acceptable. Strength, not weakness, may be the marching orders of the home. This makes it extremely difficult for a young person to process the volatile emotions of grief. For fear of punishment, children might repress feelings of anger, sadness, guilt, and loss.

In families where emotions are not openly discussed or displayed, the home becomes a mausoleum for the living— a cold crypt for the crushed in spirit. The dead person may, quite literally, become a skeleton in the family's closet. Death, grief, and mourning may be forbidden subjects that no one is permitted to experience or discuss.

On the other hand, there is also the *Ordinary People* syndrome where one or both parents glorify the life of a dead child in a way that makes it impossible for the surviving children to grieve in a healthy way. Forced to compete with the memory of the dead sibling and unable to receive comfort from inconsolable parents, children may draw into a world of their own.

Fear of the Unknown

Death is a mysterious, powerful experience. The upheaval it causes in families is tremendous, and for that reason alone, a child can become afraid of everyday situations and events. Fear of the unknown is the anxiety a child feels simply from living in an unpredictable world. It is fear for fear's sake. Like a coiled rattlesnake, the fear of the unknown springs forward in nervous thoughts and questions like, "When will Daddy be home? When will I die? Do all kids die in car accidents? Do all people die when they get sick?" The unpredictability and capricious nature of death can make children feel overwhelmed by the fear of something terrible happening when they least expect it. Natural disasters, crime and violence, and trouble in the home all contribute to a child's fear of the unknown.

Fortunately, as parents, relatives, and caregivers, there are specific and practical steps we can take to help our children deal with their fears in a healthy and constructive way.

- Take time to understand the unique personality of each one of your children.
- Talk with your children about their fears.
- Offer the comfort and reassurance of your presence.
- Read grief books and literature to better understand what your child is experiencing.
- Seek professional assistance to help you and your children process your grief.
- Do not make too many commitments after the death of a loved one in order that you might be attentive to your children's needs.
- Look beyond "acting out" behavior to identify your child's fears or needs.
- Don't punish your child for being scared.

Leaving the Light On

One of the most wonderful truths in the Bible is that God is the God of light and in him there is no darkness at all. What a great place to start in helping our children understand and deal with their fears. When you listen to your children's fears and tell them that the God of this universe knows a lot about light and darkness, you are leaving a light on for them.

The Bible is filled with hundreds of verses that speak of the brilliant light of God and the power of this light in our lives. Many children do not know—or simply forget—that God created the day and the night (Gen. 1:5). When God looked at everything he made—the night, the day, the sun, moon, and stars—he saw that it was good (Gen. 1:31). Darkness is a creative flair of God's artistry. It's the backdrop he uses to contrast the colorful beauty of his handiwork. True, but try telling that to your child when they're scared. *I don't think so.* Yet children do need to know that there is nothing inherently evil about physical darkness. Yes, when the light is flipped off in their room, the darkness can be pretty scary, but God did not make darkness to scare children.

Jesus said, "I am the light of the world. Whoever follows me will never walk in darkness, but will have the light of life" (John 8:12). Jesus' words may be confusing to a six-year-old who has to walk down a darkened hallway in the middle of the night to go to the bathroom. You can just imagine that six-year-old muttering, "This hallway is looking *very* dark to me. Jesus said if I followed him, I'd *never* walk in darkness."

As your children grow in faith, you can help them understand that they are one big, bright, sparkling blaze of blinding light. Not only did Jesus say that he is the light of the world, he also said, "You are the light of the world . . . let your light shine before men, that they may see your good deeds and praise your Father in heaven" (Matt. 5:14, 16). When children are scared, they might not exactly feel like a blazing torch of glowing light. Fear makes it hard for them to feel or sense God's love. When this happens, you have the wonderful opportunity to assure your child not only of your love but of God's unconditional love as well. Let your child know that God's perfect love can drive away all of their fears (1 John 4:18). While leaving the light on in the bathroom may lead to a slightly higher electric bill, it's pennies compared to the value of the light that has been left on in their hearts.

Helping Your Children Deal with Fear

The following ideas are practical suggestions for helping your children deal with their fears. Some of these ideas may be specific for children who've just experienced the loss of a loved one. Others are for kids who are just plain scared of the dark. Many of these ideas and suggestions came from my interview with clinical psychologist, Dr. Randi McAllister-Black. Her insights are greatly appreciated.[4]

Family schedule. It would be an understatement to say that a death in the family throws the family schedule out of whack. Being shuttled from house to house with infrequent meals and a steady flow of visitors can be upsetting to children who are used to a simpler daily schedule. Pay attention to how the recent changes are affecting your children and their sleeping patterns. Lack of sleep will make them tired, irritable, susceptible to becoming sick, and yes, vulnerable to the wide range of fears associated with death. Try to get your children back to the usual schedule as soon as possible.

Bedtime rituals. Develop a consistent nightly routine centered around a regular bedtime. A consistent schedule will help shape a child's understanding of going to bed. Putting pajamas on. Brushing teeth. Putting away clothes and toys. Tucking in bed. Reading a story. Saying prayers. All of these bedtime rituals are important to closing a child's day.

Don't tease or shame. Humiliating your children for being afraid will not help their fears. Respect their fears as real and help them to talk about what they're afraid of. Showing comfort will reassure them that they are safe in your care.

Get out the monster spray. Hold an imaginary can of "monster spray" and give one to your child as well. Spray underneath the bed, in the closet, out the window, and in the hallway. In the morning, notice how there will be no monster footprints on the carpet. Show your child your amazing discovery. Poof! No more monsters!

Tame the TV. Many childhood fears develop from what kids watch on television. As much as possible, try to prevent your child from watching scary shows on television. If they go to a friend or relative's house, find out what shows they will be watching.

Play the "what if" game. As your children tell you about their fears, help them to be resourceful by creating solutions. Ask them, "What if you were lost in a forest? What would you do if a bear chased you?" The "what if" game not only produces a lot of laughter, it shows children they can cope with their fears in positive ways.

Give your child a flashlight. Kids love flashlights. Turn out the lights and spend a few minutes making animal shadows with your hands on the wall or ceiling. Get under the covers and make a flashlight fort. A flashlight is a simple, fun distraction.

Read books. Let your children pick out two or three of their favorite books. They will grow sleepy as they look at the books in bed. Yes, they may stay up a bit later, but when they're scared, they definitely don't go to sleep quickly anyway.

Play quiet music. Popping in a children's lullaby cassette or CD will help quiet their fears through the wonderful art of distraction. Soothing music can relax your child until they drift off to "La-La Land."

Read Bible stories. The Bible is filled with stories of how people faced their fears. Read the Psalms, stories about David and Goliath, Peter walking on the water, Jesus in the Garden of Gethsemane, Jonah and the whale, and dozens of fear-filled stories of faith.

Pray with your child. Tell your child that not only do you care about their fears, but God also cares. Pray for God to comfort your child. Ask him to give your child his peace and protection. Ask God to provide courage for your child. Ask him to take his BIG, BIG foot and boot those awful monsters right out of the closet and into the stinky trash can where they will be consumed by ferocious, hungry ants. Humor is a wonderful way to melt fear.

Humor is also a great way to enjoy the crazy questions kids ask about life and death.

7

Will There Be Different Colors in Heaven?

Honest Questions from Inquisitive Kids

*P*owerhouse is a wonderful children's ministry fueled by hundreds of volunteers and church staff members who share a single passion: They want every child to experience and know the love of Jesus. Leading this massive group is Dean Lies, the director of children's ministry. Every Bible-jamming, foot-stomping, song-screaming, body-moving, verse-memorizing music program, dance class, sports events, camp, and retreat that Dean and his staff design is centered around this singular purpose. The entire children's ministry staff makes loving God a whole lot of fun.

What I really like about this ministry is that Dean and his staff are willing to talk to children about tough subjects. They are open to the kind of brain-twisting, wild, creative, and burning questions that children have. Questions about the death and eternal fate of favorite pets, the exact latitude and

longitude of heaven's expanse, the details of the daily routine and schedule inside those pearly gates, the length of
eternity, the size and dimension of our new bodies in heaven,
and what kind of food will be served at God's banquet table
(sweets only . . . no vegetables!). Most importantly, through
all the fun, crazy, and serious questions thrown their way,
Dean and his staff are helping children develop an eternal
perspective for their lives. By taking the questions seriously,
this ministry team is showing children that no question
about God's kingdom is stupid, irrelevant, or insignificant.
Every child is special. Every question is important. Every idea
is worth exploring.

On a recent winter retreat, the theme for the weekend was
"Heaven Can't Wait." The whole weekend was devoted to
teaching kids what the Bible says about heaven. During their
meeting times, the children sang songs about heaven, discussed Bible verses describing what heaven is and what it is
not, acted out various skits and short plays, and discussed
the significance of living here on earth with our eyes on
heaven. Most importantly, the children were encouraged to
ask a lot of questions about heaven.

And boy, did they have a lot of questions!

Taboo Busters

Children have a unique capacity for asking any question
that intrigues them. With one insightful, missile-like directed
question, children can easily burst any social convention or
taboo subject. Who hasn't witnessed a small child standing
among a group of adults when suddenly the child pops a
question about Mommy or Daddy's bathroom habits or
some other "forbidden" subject that sets off a roar of laughter from everyone listening?

You can be sure—what adults do not discuss in public,
children will. The topics adults find inappropriate, uncom-

fortable, or downright embarrassing to discuss are dry kindling for the burning questions in children's minds. They are thrill-seekers of the unknown, the fearless pursuers of truth, and the innocent babes of inquiry. Children are the ultimate taboo busters. (They're also a sneaky, mischievous bunch of little troublemakers—especially toddlers—but that's another subject we don't have time to deal with!)

As parents, teachers, relatives, or role models to the children and teenagers in our lives, we have the choice of either nurturing or smothering the questions young people have about life and death. We are in a unique position to help them develop a healthy understanding of death, the meaning of life, the significance of what happens in the world around them, and the best way to handle the injustices and contradictions of daily living. Ultimately, we can instill in them hearts filled with hope for this life and life after death. While we may not be able to answer every question they have, we cannot underestimate the power of listening to them and showing them how important their questions are to us.

As parents, teachers, relatives, or role models to the children and teenagers in our lives, we have the choice of either nurturing or smothering the questions young people have about life and death.

Children don't necessarily care how much we know or don't know; our knowledge doesn't impress them. They care that we care about their questions. They care that what they think is important is also what we think is important. They care that we listen to them. They care that no topic, idea, concept, issue, or question is off-limits to them.

Before We Begin, Are There Any Questions?

What follows are just some of the hundreds of honest questions about heaven, life, death, pets, and almost everything in between that were posed to Dean and his ministry team during the "Heaven Can't Wait" retreat. The scope of these questions is by no means conclusive or comprehensive. And neither are the responses. I'm sure that your kids, grandchildren, nieces, or nephews could add loads to this list. Use these questions as a launchpad for talking to your child about heaven, death, dying, and eternal life. You might even find yourself responding to your son or daughter, "That's a great question. Look, the question you just asked is right here in this book!"

The Bible provides a number of specific answers to some of these questions; as I mentioned in chapter 3, God's Word has a lot to say about life and death. On questions where the Bible is silent, where it does not provide a reasonably conclusive answer, or when it is a matter that theologians have been arguing over for thousands of years, I will provide a general response that will at least enable you to explore this subject further with your child. Some questions will be followed with Bible verses for you to talk about with your son or daughter. And on some of the zany questions, I've taken the liberty to be a kid myself and explore the possibilities that await us in heaven. In all of these questions, my hope is that you learn a little, laugh a lot, and enjoy exploring the fertile soil of your child's curiosity about all things eternal. Though it may be theologically frightening for some readers, my goal is not to provide the "perfect" answer to all of life's mysteries. God never shows all his cards. (And I hope that you would be uncomfortably suspicious if I tried to do it for him.) My goal is a whole lot simpler: I want to encourage you to begin talking with your children about these important matters. Sometimes just talking is better than having the right answer.

So without any further rambling, let's get into the hearts and minds of what kids are asking about almost everything between here and heaven.

When we're in heaven, how will my dad look—young or old?

This is a significant question, particularly for a young child whose father has died. The Bible tells us that we will receive new, glorified bodies in heaven. It makes no mention of whether or not we will age. In heaven, there will be no twenty-four-hour clock like we use to measure the time and date here on earth. From what the Bible tells us, we know that we will somehow look different because our physical bodies will remain here on earth.

Will our bodies be the same?

No, the physical body we have here on earth will stay here when we die. Our soul goes to heaven. The Bible makes a clear distinction between our physical bodies and our souls, which are invisible. Our bodies here on earth have all sorts of limitations. Our bones break. Our bodies bleed. We have times of health and times of sickness. What God promises us is a better body . . . a whole body . . . a perfect body (all those hours spent sweating at the health club finally pay off!).

What do you do for fun in heaven?

Great question, but the answer really depends on what you like to do for fun. God created you and God created fun. If you like playing football, singing fun songs, making forts, painting, reading stories, laughing, and playing fun games, then don't you think that God likes to have fun too? Think about the funnest thing you like to do here on earth, and now imagine heaven as a place that's a bazillion times funner than that. You can't even begin to imagine all the fun that God has prepared for you in heaven. Check out 1 Corinthians 2:9.

Do you have a job in heaven?

Yes, you'll have lots of jobs in heaven, but you won't have to worry about sweating a lot like your dad does when he works in the garden. In heaven, your most important job will be singing and praising God. Another job will be celebrating God at the huge banquet table he prepared for all who love him. The Bible says that we will reign with Christ (Rev. 22:5), and that implies we'll all have certain responsibilities in heaven. Whatever specific job God has in mind for us, we won't become tired, lazy, bored, or restless because the new bodies we receive will be powerful and perfect.

In heaven, will we be able to fly?

If you're tired of being grounded by gravity here on earth, you just may have an opportunity to fly in heaven, but I can't offer you any guarantees (or frequent flier miles). The Bible says that heaven will be completely different from earth, and that includes the physical realm as well. We know that the Bible says angels fly, but nowhere do we find humans performing solo aeronautical maneuvers.

Will we be able to become angels?

I'm glad you asked that question! There's a lot of confusing information here on earth about angels. First, the Bible says that humans and angels are two types of separate beings created by God. Angels do not become humans and humans do not become angels in heaven or on earth. Angels were created for the specific purpose of serving God in heaven and carrying out earthly duties as God tells them to. In heaven, we will worship and serve God with the angels, but we will not become angels because we are a unique creation of God.

Will we be able to meet Jesus and other Bible characters?

You betcha! In Matthew 25, Jesus tells three different stories of what it will be like when we meet him in heaven. Jesus also said in John 14:2–3: "In my Father's house are many rooms; if it were not so, I would have told you. I am going there to prepare a place for you. And if I go and prepare a place for you, I will come back and take you to be with me that you also may be where I am." Jesus can't wait to meet us in heaven. We will see his face (Rev. 22:4). Not only will we get to meet Jesus face to face, we will also meet everyone in his kingdom throughout history. Heaven will be a great gathering place for all of God's people.

Does heaven have any swimming pools or sports?

Heaven has something better than a swimming pool; there is a huge river flowing with the water of life. It pours right out of God's throne and flows down the main boulevard of heaven (see Rev. 22:1–2). God promises an eternity that certainly won't be boring, but he has chosen to keep some of his special surprises a secret until then. The apostle John also gives us a beautiful picture in Revelation 7:9–17 of Jesus, the Lamb of God, leading us as a shepherd to streams of living water. Are you ready to dive in?

What are we gonna wear in heaven?

God has designed the most comfortable attire of all for us in heaven . . . a white robe. That will be very different than the jeans, dresses, and T-shirts we're used to wearing. A white robe represents those who have been forgiven by Jesus Christ, having their sins washed away by his blood. Not only will we have new bodies in heaven, God has new clothes picked out for us as well. He thinks of everything, doesn't he?

What will my family be like in heaven?

Will your mom, dad, brothers, or sisters be the same in heaven as they are now? Like everything else the Bible tells us about heaven, our families as we know them here on earth will probably be different in heaven. First of all, everyone who goes to heaven will finally be perfect. That means no family problems. Second, there won't be any dirty, rotten tricks like your brother taking your bicycle without asking or your sister ripping the remote control out of your hands. Third, Mom or Dad will no longer be the boss around the house. Our heavenly Father will be the Big Boss, and all of God's people will be like one big family in heaven.

Is there really a heaven and a God?

Yes, there really is a heaven and there really is a God. The Bible is like a long letter written to you from God to let you know that he exists and that he's the one who created you. The Bible was written so you could come to know God and how much he loves you.

Why did God make the Bible and heaven so confusing?

Like any other large book, the Bible can be confusing if you're not familiar with it. However, the Bible wasn't written to be confusing. Think of the Bible as a large schoolbook with all sorts of different topics, stories, characters, poems, and adventures. At first, it takes some time to get familiar with who is who and what story goes where. Heaven is so fantastic that there is so much we can't know. But there are lots of things we can know about heaven and they are written in the Bible.

Are we perfect in heaven?

Wouldn't it be wonderful to live in a new world where you never scraped your knee, fell off your bike, never lost your favorite toy, or never had your feelings hurt by an unkind word? The Bible promises that this new world, the kingdom of heaven, will be a perfect place where nothing goes wrong. We won't become sick. We won't hurt others and others won't hurt us. We won't be afraid of the dark. We will always have peace in our hearts as we enjoy the perfect world God has made for us to enjoy him. Philippians 3:20–21 says, "But our citizenship is in heaven. And we eagerly await a Savior from there, the Lord Jesus Christ, who, by the power that enables him to bring everything under his control, will transform our lowly bodies so that they will be like his glorious body." We will be perfect just as Jesus is perfect.

What will we look like in heaven?

We're not exactly sure yet. Again and again, the Word of God says that there will be a big difference between our earthly body and our heavenly body (see 1 Cor. 15:35–55). Even John, one of Jesus' disciples, wasn't sure what we would look like in heaven. He wrote, "Dear friends, now we are children of God, and what we will be has not yet been made known. But we know that when he appears, we shall be like him, for we shall see him as he is" (1 John 3:2). We will have what the Bible calls a glorified, powerful, spiritual body (1 Cor. 15:43–44). We probably won't have the same freckles, dimples, or pudgy cheeks that Grandma likes to pinch. Come to think of it, Grandma won't have her wrinkles either.

If babies die when they are really little, will they go to heaven or hell?

Nowhere in the Bible does it say that babies go to hell. In fact, Jesus said, "Let the little children come to me, and do not hinder them, for the kingdom of heaven belongs to such as these" (Matt. 19:14). Isn't that amazing? The kingdom of heaven belongs to children. That includes babies too. Jesus also said in Matthew 18:3, "I tell you the truth, unless you change and become like little children, you will never enter the kingdom of heaven." So you see, little children are very special to Jesus. Jesus said the greatest people in the kingdom of heaven are those who become like little children.

Will we live in heaven like we do on earth?

Living in heaven will be a new experience compared to living here on earth. In this world, toys break, kids say mean things, accidents happen, and just about anything that can go wrong, does go wrong. Heaven will be completely different. In heaven, Jesus says, "I'm making everything new." That means we will have a brand-new life in heaven. Jesus has new experiences, new adventures, and special times with him awaiting us in heaven.

Where is heaven and where does it end?

Heaven actually means "up." When the Bible speaks of the place where God lives, it describes a very real place far past our solar system, our galaxy, and even past the zillions of other galaxies in outer space. To locate where heaven ends, those old galaxy maps inside *National Geographic* just won't cut it. Let's just say heaven is huge . . . a big, big place for everyone who wants to be there.

What is hell?

When people speak of heaven, they usually also bring up that other word: H-e-double-toothpicks. Hell is a place that was created not for humans but for Satan and his demons. Hell was never made for humankind. However, if there are people who hate God and do not want to follow his ways, hell is the only place for these people to spend eternity without God. The Bible describes it as a bad place reserved for people who don't want to go to heaven. Through Jesus Christ, everyone on earth can go to heaven.

Will my guinea pig, Kermit, go to heaven?

When God first created the world, humans were made to be with God and animals were made so humans would have food to eat. Humans were given a spirit, what some people call a *soul*. Animals were not. We don't know for sure if animals here on earth will be in heaven, but it's clear that God likes animals. The Bible describes all sorts of fantastic and strange-looking animals in heaven (see Revelation 4). Animals are used to describe who Jesus is—the Lamb of God, the Lion of Judah. Isaiah 11:6–9 even paints a picture of a little child leading a wolf, a lamb, a lion, a calf, a goat, and a leopard together in God's kingdom. God knows how much children love their pets. In heaven, anything will be possible.

When you go to heaven, can you see and think like you can now?

Better eyes, better brains. That's what God promises for us in heaven. On good ol' planet earth, we can only see so far and we have a tendency to forget things. We won't have that problem in heaven. With the new bodies God gives us in heaven, we will definitely be able to see better and know everything we need to know. The apostle Paul said, "Now we see a blurred image in a mirror. Then [in heaven] we will see very clearly. Now my knowledge is incomplete. Then I will have complete knowledge as God has complete knowledge of me" (1 Cor. 13:12 *God's Word*).

Do the people go to heaven that have not asked Jesus in their heart, but still do good?

That's a great question because there's a lot of people who sincerely believe that being a good person can get you into heaven. The Bible has a different perspective on whether being a good person is enough to be able to enter heaven. Psalm 53:2–3 tells how God looked down from heaven to see if there was anyone who seeks God, and he discovered that there was no one who does good (all the time), not even one. Since we have all sinned (Rom. 3:23), God sent Jesus to earth so we could have forgiveness for our sins and be able to spend eternity with him. Therefore, it is a relationship with Jesus and not goodness that determines whether a person goes to heaven or not. God has the ultimate say about who gets into heaven.

When we're in heaven, we'll remember our friends and family that we left behind and be sad. If we can't be sad in heaven, how is that possible?

When we get to heaven, there will be no sadness, no tears, no pain, and no suffering. We won't feel sadness for the family and friends we left behind because all sadness will be gone. Jesus says that the earth and all things related to it will be no more. That isn't something to be afraid of or scared about because God has wonderful things planned for us in heaven.

Do plants go to heaven like people do?

Like animals, plants are part of the natural order God created when he made the world. Without plants here on earth, we wouldn't have the oxygen we need to breathe. Our bodies in heaven won't need oxygen, so we really wouldn't need plants in heaven. Plants on earth may not necessarily *go* to heaven, but since heaven is a beautiful place, I imagine God will already have it filled with all sorts of colorful flowers, trees, and incredible new creations we've never seen here on earth.

What's a casket?

A casket is a metal or wooden box designed to hold a dead body. When a person dies, the body is placed in a casket before they are buried in a cemetery. A casket is only used for a dead body. It usually has handles on the side so it is easy to carry. Inside, caskets are often lined with a soft cloth material. (This is a good time to explain to your children the difference between the person's soul and their physical body. The person's body died, but their soul lives on.)

What's a grave?

A grave is a large hole dug in the ground to hold a dead body. Most graves are usually six or eight feet deep and four feet wide. Most dead bodies are placed in a casket before being put in a grave. Once a casket has been placed in a grave, the hole is filled in with dirt and covered on top with grass. Many people place flowers, flags, or balloons at the grave of a family member as a special way to remember them.

What's a grave marker?

Once a body has been buried in a grave, a grave marker (also called a *headstone* or *tombstone*), a large polished stone, is used to identify where the person is buried. Written on the gravestone is the person's name, date of birth, date of death, and sometimes a Bible verse, saying, or quote about the person's life. Some grave markers, especially in old cemeteries, are large and very elaborate creations. Grave markers are important because cemeteries have hundreds, even thousands of people buried in them. Without a grave marker, it would be very difficult to find where a loved one was buried.

What's a funeral?

A funeral is a time when family and friends gather together to say good-bye to a loved one who has died. A funeral can be held at a church, a mortuary, a cemetery, or a home . . . just about anywhere. Songs are sung. People stand up to talk about the person who died. Prayers are said. Sometimes, the dead person may be lying in an open casket for everyone to see. People often cry at funerals because they are sad someone they love has died. It's been said that funerals are for the living and not for the dead. Adults and children of all ages can attend a funeral. A funeral is a helpful way for children to experience the reality of their loved one's death. Funerals remind us that we, too, will someday die.

What's a cemetery?

A cemetery is a plot of land where dead people are buried. Cemeteries can be large or small. They are usually pretty places with lots of trees, green grass, and quiet places to sit. Many people visit cemeteries to go to the graves of their loved ones. Cemeteries are quiet places to remember and honor our loved ones who have died.

What's an obituary?

An obituary is an announcement of someone's death. Obituaries are usually found in newspapers, and they contain a brief biography of the person's life. They explain who the living relatives are, where and when the funeral service is being held, and what mortuary is handling the funeral arrangements.

What's a mortuary?

A mortuary is a company that takes care of a person's body once that person has died. The people who work at the mortuary prepare the body for burial or cremation. They also take care of funeral arrangements, legal papers, and other important business matters related to the death. Funerals (i.e., memorial services) are often held in the mortuary chapel. A mortuary is also called a funeral home.

What's a eulogy?

A eulogy is a speech given at a funeral, designed to honor the life of the person who died. A family member or close friend usually gives the eulogy.

What's a pallbearer?

In the Catholic church and other Christian denominations, a burial pall is a piece of velvet used to cover a coffin. It symbolizes the death of the human body. A pallbearer is someone who assists in moving a casket at a funeral. Since a casket is heavy, four to six people are usually needed to carry it.

What's a wake?

In the old days, a wake was an all-night vigil with a dead body before the burial. Today, a wake is generally referred to as a reception after a funeral. It is a time to be with the family of the person who died.

What's embalming?

Embalming is a temporary means of preserving a body for viewing purposes. A body is embalmed after a person dies so preparations for the funeral can be made. The body fluids are replaced with preservative chemicals.

What's cremation?

To cremate means to burn something to ashes. Instead of having their bodies placed in the ground, some people prefer to have their bodies cremated when they die. The dead person feels no pain when his or her body is cremated.

What's a mausoleum?

A mausoleum is a small building where an above-ground burial takes place. Instead of being buried in a grave, the dead person is placed in the mausoleum. The casket is placed in a storage vault that is locked. Mausoleums are usually found in cemeteries.

What's an autopsy?

When an accident happens and a death occurs, a medical doctor called a *coroner* examines the body to determine the exact cause of death. Autopsies are sometimes performed to help determine if the death was accidental or not.

What's a hearse?

A hearse is a car used to transport a casket. Sometimes the casket is taken to the church for a funeral service. At other times, the hearse takes the casket directly to the cemetery. It is most common for hearses to be either black, white, or brown.

Why does Uncle Harry look so different in the casket?

To prepare a body for viewing purposes, it is common to use makeup. Uncle Harry's face may look waxy or pale. He may not even look like the real Uncle Harry because of the makeup he has on.

What is a widow or a widower?

A widow is a woman whose husband has died. A widower is a man whose wife has died.

For families who've lost a mother or father due to a terminal illness, the reality of losing a spouse or a parent goes beyond simple definitions. Read on . . .

8

Mommy's Very Sick

Living and Dying with a Terminal Illness

I am praying my wife will not die, and friends of mine are
praying about whether they should buy a new home or not.

Todd Dean

*I*n the spring of 1992, Melitta Slaught was accidentally el-
bowed in her left breast. When the pain didn't go away, she
made an appointment with a radiologist to go in for a routine mammogram. Since her father had died of cancer when
she was twelve, Melitta wanted to make sure nothing suspicious was going on inside of her.

Accompanied by her husband, Ken, Melitta learned from
the radiologist that the mammogram showed nothing wrong
with her left breast. However, a lump had been discovered
in her right breast, and the radiologist strongly recommended that an immediate biopsy be taken.

In the brief span of one and a half hours, Melitta Slaught
went from having a simple medical procedure to meeting

with a surgeon who confirmed her worst fear: A very aggressive form of breast cancer had developed in her right breast. To arrest the cancer's growth, Melitta's oncologist recommended an immediate mastectomy followed by a particularly heavy schedule of chemotherapy. What most patients take in four or five months of chemotherapy, Melitta squeezed into three months.

During those next three months, as Ken and Melitta educated themselves about the many issues surrounding life with cancer, they also made an intentional effort to educate their two sons, Tanner and Crosby, about Melitta's illness. As expected, Tanner and Crosby had a lot of questions about cancer. Questions like: "What's cancer? Where does it come from? How does the medicine work? How do you get rid of it?" In order to help the boys understand what was happening to their mother, Ken and Melitta made their best effort to answer Tanner and Crosby's questions and to keep them completely informed during the treatment process.

Three months after the chemotherapy treatments ended, an amazing thing occurred: Melitta, very unexpectedly, became pregnant. The doctors had previously told her that the chemotherapy would send her into menopause. Future children were out of the question.

Ken, Melitta, their family, and friends embraced this miraculous event as a sign that the cancer was gone. Since it was thought to be impossible for her to have children after such rigorous chemotherapy, when Melitta did become pregnant, her doctors saw no reason why she shouldn't have the child. Besides, with pregnancy changing the blood chemistry, it would be impossible for the doctors to do any blood work to test for further signs of cancer.

On September 23, 1993, Melitta gave birth to a healthy baby boy, Casey Martin Slaught. A few days after Casey was born, despite the excitement and joy of a miraculous birth, Melitta didn't feel quite right. She wasn't recovering from the birth as quickly as she had expected.

Doctors performed a series of blood tests, and on the day the results came back, Ken received an urgent phone call at the office. Melitta's blood work was "off the charts," and she was dangerously close to cardiac arrest. Ken drove home immediately, picked up Melitta, and took her to the hospital, where she was admitted to the cardiac unit.

After another series of tests and an ultrasound, the doctors confirmed what both Ken and Melitta suspected: The cancer had returned to her body like a rushing stampede.

Melitta refused to go through chemotherapy again. If she was going to die, Melitta reasoned, she was going to live life to the fullest and not allow the chemotherapy to weaken her any more than she already was.

Seeking an alternative solution, Ken and Melitta went to New York City for a series of holistic treatments with the hope of somehow eliminating the cancer. In the weeks that followed the alternative treatment, Melitta only became weaker and weaker. The cancer began shutting down her major organs, leaving her powerless against its attack. Only six weeks after giving birth to her third son, Melitta died at home on a Friday night with Ken at her side.

Living Terminal Velocity

Living and dying with a terminal illness is an almost unreal experience. Ask any person, family member, or close friend who is suffering from cancer, leukemia, or AIDS (we all know the list is much longer than this), and you'll hear responses like:

"I can't believe this is happening."
"This is not real."
"Parents are not supposed to outlive their children."
"This is a living hell."

"I don't know how I make it through each day."

"I sometimes think this is an awful dream. When I wake up, everything will be fine."

The numbing shock and disbelief after the discovery of a terminal illness is overwhelming. Terminal illnesses flood our world with a rush of powerful emotions, difficult choices, financial worries, unresolved issues, unmet expectations, major lifestyle changes, and dark fears about the future.

Children with cancer. Fathers with diabetes. Mothers with brain tumors. A friend with AIDS. Terminal illnesses ferret deep into the core of our conscience about what we believe to be right, just, and fair. Not only do they complicate our lives in exponential ways, terminal illnesses bring our somewhat normal lives to a jolting and sudden stop. Every stitch, every thread of what we know, think, do, and believe comes unraveled as we consider the impending death of someone we love. As their life slows to a stop, our life seems to stop as well.

What makes the experience of a terminal illness so unreal is that at the same time our life seems to stop, we are also catapulted into a fast-forward series of choices, changes, and issues that tests us like never before. Life can become a frenzied pace of living at what I call "terminal velocity." Everything around us is spinning, rushing, moving too fast for us to get oriented to what is actually happening. It's as if we try to cram all the future years our loved one won't be with us in the short span of three, six, or maybe twelve months. There is so much to say, do, and experience with the person who is sick. Yet when a terminal illness drains the strength and vitality of our loved one, our expectation of living our lives to the fullest with them before they die must often be adjusted. Our world suddenly becomes very small as it is knocked sideways with the desperate need to live so much more of life with so little time.

As I write this chapter, jumping around in my mind are images of people I have known who've died from terminal illnesses. My best friend, Dana Robinson. My cousin Kenny's wife, Melitta. Charlotte Dean, the wife of an old friend and ministry cohort, Todd. It's impossible to live on this planet very long without having someone close to you die of cancer or some other terminal illness.

If we're going to talk to our children about death, dying, and eternal life, then sooner or later the subject of terminal illness will come up. Every year, hundreds and thousands of children witness their mom, dad, brother, sister, relative, or friend go through the slow, torturous process of dying from a terminal illness. The lifestyle issues, tough choices, and realities a family must live with when a family member is dying are unique. The issues regarding terminal illnesses are not the same as deaths resulting from heart attacks, strokes, accidents, suicides, or murders. Every illness, accident, and tragedy is unique and needs to be treated as such.

Though whole books—even volumes of books—have been written dedicated to the topic of terminal illnesses, I have a few short pages to write about this very complex and difficult subject. Though limited, I hope you find this information useful. The main purpose of this chapter is to give you a brief sketch of the unique needs and issues facing a family dealing with terminal illness. This chapter is written with patients, families, and most of all, children in mind.

Before we explore this important topic, for clarity's sake, I would like to note that there is a significant difference between a chronic and a terminal illness. For example: Most forms of cancer are chronic, but as we know, not all cancer is terminal. There are many people living healthy lives years after being diagnosed and treated for cancer. Though some issues will be similar in dealing with a chronic and a terminal illness, this chapter will only deal with the subject of terminal illness—that is, people whose disease has given them a very short time to live.

A Long Process of Loss

When Charlotte Dean was diagnosed with brain cancer, she and her family began a long process of loss. The dreams, hopes, and aspirations she had shared with her husband, Todd, were put on hold in order to focus on her immediate and necessary medical treatment. Her surgeries, radiation, and chemotherapy treatments stole time away from playing with her two children, Josh and Sarah. The simple, everyday tasks like going to the mall, shopping at the grocery store, and visiting friends came to a complete stop when she lost her ability to drive. As her illness progressed, Charlotte began forgetting names, places, and special memories. Soon, she became confined to a wheelchair as she lost her physical mobility. Like the thousands of families who witness the gradual decline of a loved one's health, Todd and his family began the long process of loss the moment she was diagnosed with cancer.

Families living with a terminal illness bear the unique and constant burden of enduring loss after loss long before a loved one dies. There is the loss of normalcy in everyday living. There is the loss of feeling healthy and loss of the freedom to do anything one wants. There is the loss of dreams and hopes for the future. There is the loss of emotional and sexual intimacy. There is the loss of identity. Mom isn't just Mom anymore. She is *Mom with cancer.* Dad isn't just Dad anymore. He is *Dad with pancreatic cancer.*

In addition to these losses, the powerful effects of chemotherapy also lead to the loss of physical beauty. Cancer drugs often cause loss of hair, swollen facial and body features, or extreme weight loss. Financial and material loss also enters into the picture when families cash in homes, cars, jewelry, pension plans, IRAs, stock, and anything else of value to pay for medical treatment. Physical mobility. Careers. Security. Exercise. Friends. Self-esteem. The list goes on and on. As family and friends watch the disease ravage the sick person's body, hope slowly begins to evaporate with the harsh truth that this person is going to die.

As the adult family and friends try to cope with the terminal illness, children also experience a powerful sense of loss. A father with a terminal illness may not be able to wrestle on the ground with his kids anymore. Mom may be unable to attend school plays or athletic events because all her time is now spent at the hospital. When a brother or sister becomes terminally ill, children experience the loss of playing with their sibling. Children lose a sense of security as the adults around them begin talking about selling the house, moving away, or sending the children off to live with relatives. Depending on the illness and the specific family characteristics, some children may lose family vacations, movie nights, stories at bedtime, hugs, long walks, and all the delightful adventures they experienced before the illness entered their lives.

Families living with a terminal illness bear the unique and constant burden of enduring loss after loss long before a loved one dies.

Unresolved Issues

What many families unexpectedly face when confronted with the painful period of watching a loved one die in agony are unresolved issues of the past. It is not uncommon for unresolved traumas, family history issues, previous losses, and broken relationships to be revisited at the time of a terminal illness.

Given enough time and enough tragedy, this life can rub people raw. As if life isn't hard enough already, terminal illnesses can trigger buried emotions, unexplored issues, and hidden agendas. When a terminal illness strikes a family, the family brings to the illness its coping mechanisms, assumptions and expectations, beliefs and values, patterns of interaction, faith traditions, methods of communication, past history, and present conflicts. In other words, when a family member becomes sick, a whole lot of other stuff can surface.

In my interviews with psychologists who work with terminally sick patients and their families, I learned that in addition to helping families deal with the immediate crisis of the terminal sickness, much of their work is spent helping families deal with the critical life issues that surfaced as a result of the sickness.

When dealing with children who have terminal illnesses, parents are confronted with many of the unresolved issues of their own past. For instance, a parent who has never attended a funeral may be fearful of attending a son or daughter's funeral. Terminal illnesses may deepen already existing conflicts in the marriage relationship. A spouse receiving counseling from a social worker regarding a child's illness may also ask questions regarding how to handle marital conflicts or strained relationships with extended family members. In other cases, some parents may feel inclined to spoil or allow themselves to be manipulated by their sick child out of feelings of guilt or sadness over the child's illness.

Issues of guilt, anger, abuse, denial, sibling rivalry, jealousy, loss, or any unresolved events or traumas of the past can come charging forward to the present when a terminal illness is diagnosed. Dr. Randi McAllister-Black, a clinical psychologist with the City of Hope in Duarte, California, states, "The issues a family brings into the diagnosis can profoundly affect the adjustment to the diagnosis and treatment of serious illness."[5]

She further states that families that are aware of their past histories, struggles, faith tradition, communication and conflict patterns, and current issues are poised to weather the difficulty of a serious illness a bit smoother than families who are not aware of their family dynamics.

Constant and Difficult Choices

"How are we supposed to live when we go from MRI to MRI," Todd Dean once remarked to me over the telephone. An insightful question. There are an infinite number of very personal and difficult choices a family faces when dealing with a terminal illness.

What are our medical treatment options?

How are we going to meet the emotional, physical, and spiritual needs of each family member?

Is our life insurance policy current?

How are we going to explain this to the kids?

Should we move?

Should we take a new job in another city?

Is it wise to get a two-year car lease if we're not sure I'll be alive next year?

How are we going to pay for all the costs our insurance doesn't cover?

If my husband dies, will I have to return to work?

What prior commitments and plans do we have to cancel or rearrange?

If we take a vacation, is there a good hospital nearby?

Should we go for another round of radiation or more chemotherapy?

How should we say good-bye?

How will this illness affect our daily schedule and quality of life?

Should we use every medical means to prolong life as long as possible?

What are we going to do for funeral arrangements?

What legal and custodial issues need to be addressed?

Do we understand the difference between General Power of Attorney and Durable Power of Attorney for Health Care?

One resource I highly recommend for every family dealing with a terminal illness is an excellent book entitled *Dying 101: A Short Course on Living for the Terminally Ill.* In bold language, the authors deal with the many difficult issues and options for terminally ill individuals and their families. *Dying 101* is not so much about dying as it is how one chooses to spend the rest of life. (See resource section for ordering information.)

As you can see, a family dealing with a terminal illness faces extremely difficult questions and choices. I listed just a few. Just as the grief process is tough and confusing, so is the painful process of watching a loved one die. There is nothing simple about a terminal illness. Terminal illnesses cost money. They cost time. They cost relationships. No matter how strong the family, no matter how solid a person's faith or inner resolve, terminal illnesses can drain every physical, emotional, financial, and spiritual resource. While family members devote enormous amounts of time and attention to caring for their dying relative, they must also live with the realization that the majority of people they know continue to live their normal, everyday lives. I'll never forget Todd Dean summarizing this harsh reality when he said, "I am praying my wife will not die, and friends of mine are praying about whether they should buy a new home or not."

Kids Included

There are many aspects of the adult world in which children are not allowed to participate. Adult parties. Amusement park rides with four-foot height requirements. Athletic clubs. Space shuttle rides. You get the picture. Terminal illnesses present a major education into the reality of death which everyone will face. When an illness results in death, an indelible imprint is stamped on the soul of every family member. For this reason (and many others), children need to be included in the whole process of a terminal illness. By explaining what the problem is, what type of illness it is, what the method of treatments are, how the family's lifestyle may be affected, what symptoms can be expected, what the possible consequences are, how long the hospital stays will be, and how all of this is difficult and upsetting, parents position themselves to interact with their children in a very valuable way. By taking the time to explain what is happening, parents will discover what their children's questions are and how to appropriately respond.

As I mentioned in a previous chapter, we need to be careful about the words we use to explain difficult concepts to children. Explaining that Daddy has a very serious illness to three children ages nine, six, and three will be met with three very different interpretations of what this really means. Also, children will have different reactions to a terminal illness depending on who in the family is sick. A whole series of different issues may be present if it is a sibling who is terminally ill. For a child whose brother or sister is dying, it is not uncommon for the healthy child to feel jealous of all the attention their sick sibling is receiving. Comments like, "I wish I was sick so I could get so many presents," or "I wish they would just die," often stem from a child's unmet needs for time, love, and attention. Such thoughts and comments are often followed by intense feelings of guilt and remorse.

The degree to which children are informed, educated, and included in the issues surrounding the terminal illness can greatly affect how they handle their grief after the person dies. If children have been taught to stuff their feelings and not to ask any questions about a sick relative, it shouldn't be surprising to see negative behavior patterns arise in the months and years that follow the death of a loved one. In fact, a frequent theme I encountered in my research for this book was adults who had never been informed or included in the dying and grieving process as children themselves. I read interview after interview of adults who had never dealt with the process of death and their feelings of loss for a loved one who had died during their childhood. Now, as adults, they were sifting through years of buried, untouched grief and the negative behavior patterns that had developed as a result of not being allowed to express their feelings and emotions as a child.

When you actively include your children by helping them understand what a terminal illness is and how it will affect the whole family, you can expect a lot of questions! A few questions you might just hear are:

"What does 'terminal' mean?"

"Why is Daddy tired all the time?"

"When is Mommy coming home from the hospital?"

"How come my sister gets so many presents and I don't get any?"

"How come we never have fun anymore?"

"Is Grandpa going to die?"

"Why did we pray so much if Daddy didn't get better?"

"Who is going to take care of me if you die too?"

These are just a few of the questions from the children of families I interviewed for this book. You can expect to hear these and many more. However, don't let your child's innocent and important questions scare you into thinking you have to have the right answer. In most cases, you won't, and that's okay. Your job is to explain to your children what you do know, and to give them the safest, loving care you can. Don't tell your children lies or make promises that you can't keep. By just knowing what is going on, children can begin to cope with what they have been told. Children can be amazingly resilient with what is entrusted to them. When you include your children in the living and dying process of a terminal illness, you are being the best parent you can be. Even though dealing with a terminal illness is a tremendously difficult experience, you can at least be assured that you are not abandoning your children to their unspoken thoughts and feelings.

> *When you include your children in the living and dying process of a terminal illness, you are being the best parent you can be.*

Depending on the age of your children and the type of terminal illness a family member has, you need to determine what is appropriate for them to know. Some forms of cancer are physically devastating, and it is probably not critical for your children to know the explicit details of what the cancer will do. While it is not necessary to be excessively graphic, it is essential to be truthful in explaining the severity of the illness. For a family member dying of an AIDS related illness, it is important for a child to have correct information about the disease. Whether the terminal illness is cancer, AIDS, leukemia, lupus, cystic fibrosis, multiple sclerosis, or any other degenerative disease, never underestimate the importance of a clear and understandable explanation of the illness. Again, in cases like these, I am not speaking of chronic illnesses, like the many forms of cancer that can be effectively treated, but terminal illnesses.

Welcome! Please Leave Your Fears at the Door

So read the sign that Ken posted at the front door of their home in Santa Barbara, California. One of the difficulties Ken and Melitta faced as her illness worsened was knowing how to deal with friends who came to visit with terror in their eyes. "For the person with cancer," Ken described, "often the last thing they want or need is to meet with people who are afraid to talk about the illness. A person with cancer wants to be with people who are 'up' and positive."

While a terminal illness can trigger fears of death, it's important not to project those fears onto the person who is terminally ill. Though their body is being destroyed by a deadly disease, the terminally ill person is still alive. *They still have a life.* Most people who are terminally ill don't want anyone to pity them. They want to be treated with dignity and respect like any other healthy human being.

As we conclude this brief chapter on understanding the unique needs of families dealing with a terminal illness, let's look at a few specific ways to help them in this difficult process.

- Be sensitive to the needs of the whole family, not just the person who is sick.
- Offer practical help with chores, shopping for food, or taking care of children.
- Write a letter instead of buying a generic greeting card.
- Be aware of your own feelings about life and death.
- Don't be offended if your request to visit is turned down. Depending on the stage of the illness, a sick person may need a lot of rest or may simply want to be alone.
- Be careful not to overstay your welcome.
- Be a good listener. Talk about whatever the sick person wants to talk about. The illness is probably not the only thing on their mind.

- If appropriate, offer them financial assistance. Most people are reluctant to talk about this sensitive issue, but if there is a true need, financial assistance is a very practical way to help.
- Be aware of the sick person's feelings about their physical appearance. They may feel very self-conscious about how they look.
- When appropriate, offer to pray and read Scripture with them.
- Don't offer explanations for their illness by explaining God's will or the limitations of modern science. This will not help.
- Keep in touch with the sick person through notes, phone calls, and visits.
- Find out if there are important upcoming dates or family events such as birthdays, school plays, or school vacations. They may especially need help during the holidays.
- Offer to take the kids out for an evening of miniature golf or the movies.
- If appropriate, ask the sick person if they have any special requests for the funeral or memorial service.
- Assure the sick person of your best thoughts and prayers.

Just as understanding the unique needs of a family dealing with a terminal illness can be a difficult process, so too is discerning the special needs of teenagers wrestling with grief. Though many young people may give the appearance of not wanting help with their grief, there are plenty of struggling teenagers who secretly wish they had someone to pour out their heart to. That person just may be you . . .

9

Nobody Gets outta Here Alive

Talking with Your Teenager

> There is no party Death does not crash. There is no time she does not shadow. And the only way we blunt and cover her presence is by dancing a blind denial. She is here. Wherever there is life. Death walks the boundaries.
>
> Walter Wangerin Jr.

*E*very year we receive piles of colorful Christmas cards from friends and family near and far. I'll never forget the letter we received last year from John and Margaret Snyder. Margaret usually writes long and detailed glimpses of the previous year, recapping the family highlights and the adventures of her three children—sixteen-year-old Jake, fourteen-year-old Jamie, and ten-year-old Jed. Always written in a fun, free-flowing style, Margaret's letters are enjoyable to read, her humor and wit leaping off the page as if she were telling the story straight to your face.

This Christmas letter was different. Drastically different. It was the last place I ever thought I'd find two stories of loss, pain, sadness, and death.

Margaret recounts the story of returning home in the middle of July with John after a ten-day vacation. Shortly after their arrival, Jamie, her teenage daughter, burst into the bedroom with the news that two of Jake's good friends had been killed an hour earlier in an automobile accident.

Fifteen minutes later, the phone rang again. It was the wife of their pastor, calling to ask Margaret to pray for a little girl named Avery Brady, a four-year-old who had been sucked underwater and held down by the drain of the Jacuzzi. At that very moment, Avery was being flown by helicopter to a hospital.

Tragically, the doctors were unable to save Avery's life. She died two days later. Going from a relaxing vacation to feeling virtually helpless at the deaths of three family friends, the Snyder family entered into a painful period of anguish and grief.

Why a chapter dedicated to teenagers? Because of peer pressure, gangs, sexual promiscuity, suicide, drugs, and alcohol, teenagers today are at an increased risk for potentially fatal activities. They also receive that little card which is every parent's worst fear: a driver's license.

More importantly, teenagers are open and willing to talk about matters of life and death. If you have young children, this may be a chapter you'll want to earmark until your kids become teenagers. If you do have a teenager who is suffering from the loss of a family member or friend at school, I hope you find this information useful.

Adolescence is tough enough without having to lose your closest friends. This turbulent period in a young person's life is marked by a seemingly endless series of changes and challenges. Middle school. High school. New friends. Identity formation. Peer pressure. Drugs and alcohol. Dating and the discovery of the opposite sex. Academic and athletic competition. Zits. Part-time jobs. Rebellion. Getting a driver's license. The intense need to be accepted by friends. And all the questions: "Who am I? Who do others think I am? Who is God? Does he really love me? What is this life all about? What happens to me when I die?"

When a best friend, brother, sister, parent, or relative dies, some teenagers wonder if God has some type of personal vendetta against them. Why would God impose what appears to be a death sentence of pain and suffering at such an important time in their lives? Death, the end of life and growth, runs exactly opposite to all of a teenager's future dreams, plans, and hopes.

> *When a best friend, brother, sister, parent, or relative dies, some teenagers wonder if God has a personal vendetta against them.*

Rock and Roll Will Never Die

Adolescence is marked by feelings of invincibility, powerful urges, and periods of rapid growth. So strong is a young person's sense of opportunity and potential that nothing—no obstacle or challenge—seems impossible. Adolescence, by its very nature, seems to be eternal. Neil Young's rock anthem, "Hey, hey, my, my . . . rock and roll will never die," speaks for every teenager's desire to take a deep, refreshing drink from the bubbling, eternal fountain of youth.

Like slamming on the brakes of an Indy car rocketing at two hundred miles an hour, the death of a loved one throws a young person's life into a careening, painful spin of confusion and insecurity. Numbed by shock, all of their opportunities, possibilities, and aspirations suddenly don't seem as relevant or important. The bubbling fountain of youth has now become a dry wasteland of despair. Never are young people more challenged than when someone they know and love dies. Never do they need more love, support, and encouragement from adults who care.

After working with teenagers in Southern California for over ten years, I have discovered the powerful influence death has in the life of a young person. Always focused on the present, many young people experiment with drugs and alcohol, thinking, "Death? I won't die until I'm ninety. It'll never happen to me while I'm young." So when a death actually does occur, what happens? The death of a loved one makes teenagers stop and think. Though stereotyped as a group of angry, rebellious Generation Xers, I've found teenagers to be particularly open to spiritual matters when they are hurting and broken over the death of someone they loved.

*The death of a loved one makes
teenagers stop and think.*

What's a Parent to Do?

So how do you talk with your teenage son or daughter about death, dying, and eternal life? Sounds like a weighty task, doesn't it?

Developing honest and open communication with teenagers is not an impossible task. Especially if you're willing to take on tough topics. Why? Because teenagers are filled with tons of thoughts, ideas, and questions about subjects that even most adults don't feel comfortable talking about.

Believe it or not, as a parent of a teenager, you stand to gain your son's or daughter's trust and respect by your willingness to talk about something you may not have all the answers to. Ask any group of teenagers whose house they love to visit and you'll discover that it is the home with adults who are willing to talk to them about anything and everything.

Sitting down and speaking with your teenagers about the reality of death and the practical implications of their decisions is one way to help nurture their spiritual, emotional, physical, social, and intellectual development. Not only are you preparing them for the future, you are helping them understand the importance of handling the challenges they face each day. You are playing a vital part in shaping their understanding of God, the realities of this life, and the life to come.

Understanding death, dying, and eternal life is just one topic among many that needs to be on your "Top 10 Talks" list for your teenagers. If you really want to earn the ear, the heart, and the respect of your teenagers, you can begin by actively preparing and equipping them not only for adolescence but for their future life as adults by having an honest discussion about these ten vital areas of life development.

Top 10 Talks with My Teenager

1. Choosing good friends
2. Sexual development, dating, and sexual choices
3. Spiritual growth and development
4. Identity and self-esteem
5. Peer pressure
6. How to manage and resolve conflict
7. Personal talents, abilities, dreams, and goals
8. Drug and alcohol abuse
9. Financial management
10. Death, dying, and eternal life

When your teenagers see your willingness to answer their questions about sexuality, peer pressure, the future, or even practical ways to handle a job interview, they'll be much more open to talking about life and death. You may even hear your teenagers boldly saying to their friends, "My parents talk with me about everything. They aren't afraid to talk about *anything*."

Coming Alongside

You may be thinking, "Talk with my teenager about all these subjects? I can't even get him to tell me what time it is! I'd have better odds speaking with Cro-Magnon man." Talking about sensitive subjects with your son or daughter may be a little intimidating, especially if your relationship is characterized by poor communication. You might think you lack credibility in their eyes. You may even feel guilty about mistakes made in the past. You might be tempted to believe, "It's too late. My teenager will never open up to me." But it is never too late to speak with your teenager about their grief or their questions about death and dying. You don't have to be a perfect parent. You don't have to be an expert on a subject that scares most people to d . . . let's just say "a lot."

Though they may be scared to ask for help, many teenagers appreciate when someone who sincerely cares comes alongside them. Your teenagers need you to listen. They also need to know that you don't have all of life figured out yet (at least, let's hope you don't!). Let your son or daughter know that you also have a lot of questions about life and death. That way, you can enter a conversation together on level ground. Heart to heart. Come with a desire to listen instead of instruct. Come with a spontaneous willingness to hear what may sound like crazy, even goofball ideas. You may be surprised what your teenagers tell you. Or what they ask you.

A word of caution: Nothing causes a young person to shut down quicker than when they sense they are not being taken seriously. Teenagers are sensitive to rejection. They are in a critical developmental stage of testing ideas, thoughts, and feelings about life. They want to be treated with dignity and respect.

Your teenagers have a strong need to be accepted as special people with unique thoughts and ideas. Winning their trust means valuing their opinions regardless of whether you agree with them or not. By coming alongside your teenagers to listen and accept what they say, you communicate the critically important unconditional message, "I love you. Your thoughts, ideas, and feelings are important to me."

Riding the Wild Waves of Grief

In her excellent grief recovery book for teenagers, *Will I Ever Feel Good Again*? Karen Dockrey takes teenagers on an insightful journey of the various thoughts and feelings they may experience during the different stages of grief. Using personal insights, Scripture, and stories of how other teenagers dealt with death and grief, she provides numerous creative exercises for them to identify and respond to their grief.

In particular, Dockrey explains the key emotions of grief— shock, sadness, guilt, anger, and depression—as a series of unpredictable waves. Teenagers will experience certain waves of emotion stronger than others depending on the circumstances of the death and their relationship to the person who died. As Dockrey points out, "Grief comes in waves. Some waves are flutters of sadness you barely feel. Other waves are so high and jolting you think they'll overpower you."[6]

Working through grief is a process, and as Dockrey notes, teenagers who are willing to work through their grief can experience wholeness and healing. PJ Kerr is an excellent example of one teenager who finally made it through the long, dark tunnel of grief.

PJ's Story

Six months after his father died from a brain tumor, seventeen-year-old PJ Kerr found himself riding the powerful, churning wave of anger. PJ explained that the anger wasn't so much because his father had died but because of all the unresolved issues and unanswered questions he had to face after his father's death. His parents had divorced when he was young, and now, as a teenager, he discovered a number of startling truths about his father.

Only a few months prior to his death, PJ's father told him that he had remarried years earlier. To PJ's surprise, he learned he had a stepmother and a stepsister he never knew existed. In the final months of his father's life, PJ not only had to wrestle with the loss of his father but also with the knowledge that his father had lied to him. *I'm old enough and mature enough to handle having a new family. Why didn't he trust me with this secret?* PJ wondered.

After his father's death, PJ was understandably angry. At the funeral, PJ didn't cry. Nor did he so much as shed a single tear in the months to follow. All he felt toward his father was extreme anger. He didn't want to talk or even think about his dad. In his words, PJ says, "I had friends, school, work, church—stuff to keep me busy." And PJ, like many teenagers, stuffed his anger deep into the dark shaft of grief. When friends and family asked how he was doing, PJ's typical, guarded response was, "I'm OK. I'm fine."

Eight months later, PJ dreamed he was in a home at the Colorado River, a place he had vacationed many times before with his father. After spending the day fishing, water-skiing, and jet-skiing, PJ returned to the home along the river. Opening the door, he called, "Dad, where are you? Dad, are you here? Dad, where are you?" No one returned his call. The home was silent. Empty.

When he awoke, PJ realized, "Oh my gosh, my dad isn't here. He's dead. This person was my *father.* He always called me his best friend. I've lost my best friend and my dad at the same time. I haven't even grieved about this yet." That's when PJ started to cry.

After his dream, PJ began to be a little bit more honest with his feelings. He still had a lot of anger toward his father, but at least he was willing to deal with his feelings. He wondered why his father hadn't trusted him with the knowledge of his stepmother and stepsister. He grieved over the fact that he wasn't given the chance to be a part of his father's new married life. He struggled with whether or not he should forgive his father for lying to him.

Finally, after having a talk with his youth pastor and spending a long time thinking about his anger, PJ went down to the beach to pray. As he sat by himself on a bench watching the glowing sun go down over the ocean, PJ sensed God telling him, "PJ, it's time for you to forgive him."

PJ describes his next feelings: "I felt a sudden calmness and then I said, 'Okay, Dad, I forgive you. You have secrets you didn't want me to know. I accept that. I'm letting go of my anger, hostility, and questions. I'm going to move on and live my life.'"

PJ added, "I said it out loud and I meant it."

Returning to School

After Avery Brady's death, her brother, Buddy, received a phone call from a friend who grilled him about the details of her Jacuzzi accident. His mother, Clarise, shares what happened next: "I didn't know this was going on at the time, but it totally distressed him. I taught Buddy to be ready to respond to insensitive questions the way I had learned—to simply say, 'I'm not comfortable talking about that.'

"When it was time to return to junior high school six weeks later, I knew Buddy was concerned about the questions he might have to field. I went in a few days before school started and spoke to both his teacher and his principal. His teacher agreed that Buddy would come in an hour late the first day, giving her a chance to discuss his situation with the class.

She asked them to consider what it would be like to be in his shoes, and what they would or would not want other kids to say to them. She then helped them discern which 'answers' were appropriate. I let her know specifically that he would not want to be asked questions about the details of his sister's accident.

"Buddy knew that this was going on and appreciated it. When he came home from school the first day, he was really glad nobody had grilled him. He said everyone treated him 'just like he was normal.'"

And that's exactly what most young people want . . . *to be treated normal.* Teenagers are very sensitive to other people's perception of them. They don't want to be treated weird by condescending adults. Like anyone else, teenagers especially don't like being embarrassed in front of their peers.

After Buddy had been harshly confronted by an insensitive and probing friend on the phone, Clarise Brady made a wise move by contacting her son's school before Buddy faced another round of potentially harmful interrogations. With a little initiative and sensitivity to her son's feelings, Clarise did what all parents can do to help their teenagers through the difficult situations that arise after a death occurs.

In her excellent article, "Sibling Grief: How Parents Can Help the Child Whose Brother or Sister Has Died," Marcia G. Scherago outlines a number of critical elements to take into consideration for children and teenagers returning to school after the death of a sibling. The following article is reprinted with permission.

> School is like a second family to children. Returning to that family after the death of their sister or brother will probably be difficult, but there are some things you can do to help make the experience positive and supportive rather than negative.
> • Prepare your children for questions and remarks. Other children are likely to ask pointed questions. They are cu-

rious and they want explanations and answers. And they are not likely to be considerate of your children's feelings. Discussing possible questions and answers with your children may be helpful. Also tell them that they can refuse to answer any questions they don't want to answer—questions that are too private or too difficult.

- Contact a favorite teacher. Explain the situation and ask for help in lending support to your child. Ask if the teacher would be willing to meet with your child to offer encouragement and to show acceptance for whatever state the child is in. Be sure the teacher understands that you don't want the child to be encouraged to put up a false front, the "stiff upper lip" approach which tends to suppress grief and avoid the healing process. After their first meeting, suggest further meetings if it seems they are helping.

- Contact the school counselor or social worker. Again explain the situation and ask for help. It would not be unreasonable in many cases to ask that your child have a visit with this person once a week for a while, then perhaps once a month. Such long-term support may help your child through an important transition, such as into a new grade or new school, a change made more difficult because of the loss. Even if your child drops out of regular visits, a resource relationship may have been established which may be used when the need is felt.

- Inquire whether there is a support group of bereaved children [teenagers].

Meeting with other students who have had similar losses can be very helpful. Feelings are easier to share in such a group. If your school does not have a support group, perhaps you can help to get one started.[7]

Helping Grieving Teenagers

Just as PJ's and Buddy's stories are unique, so is the story and experience of every teenager who loses a loved one. Teenagers need to be allowed to go through the grief experience at their own pace. They don't want to be preached at. They don't want to be told what they should or shouldn't feel. They don't want to be doted over and treated like children. Nor can they be expected to "grow up and act like an adult."

If you have a grieving teenager, the following ideas and suggestions will help you help them work through their grief at their own pace. Though you can't do your son's or daughter's grief work for them, you can provide the listening, support, and encouragement they need at this very vulnerable and painful time in their lives.

Examine the "big picture." At any given time, teenagers are facing a number of struggles in the growing process toward adulthood. The death of a loved one may be just another loss (albeit a very significant one) in a series of recent losses. Consider the other losses your teenager might have recently experienced—the loss of a boyfriend or girlfriend, the loss of a contest or competition, loss of confidence from an embarrassing situation, a disappointing grade, or a recent fight with a best friend. To an adult, these losses or disappointments may seem insignificant, but to a young person, they can be HUGE. Don't minimize any loss your teenager has recently experienced. All losses are significant.

Give your teenagers space. Giving your teenagers space doesn't mean allowing them to do anything they please. There is often a very thin emotional line between a teenager saying, "Mom, Dad . . . I'm fine," to the frustrated-stomp-off-and-slam-the-bedroom-door scream, "Just leave me alone!" Don't force your son or daughter to talk or share their feelings. If they want to be quiet and introspective, give them the time and space to do so. If they want to talk with you, include them in your space as you both work through your grief.

Expect a wave of emotions. Just like any other age group, teenagers will experience shock, guilt, anger, sadness, denial, or bitterness over the death of a loved one. Particularly with the death of a close friend, a young person may feel isolated and alone with their feelings. Your son's or daughter's cry of "You just don't understand" may be the most truthful thing they say when you try to offer comfort and support. Each teenager's grief is unique. The various moods and emotions they experience need to be accepted and validated for what they are. Don't place moral judgments on how your teenager feels.

Be aware of negative behaviors. Sometimes a young person's grief is so intense and painful that destructive, attention-getting behavior is the only way they know how to get the comfort and attention they need. Questionable friendships. Drug and alcohol abuse. Sexual promiscuity. Long periods of isolation and depression. Skipping school. Complete abandonment of previously important commitments, like athletic teams, school activities, and youth ministry events. Suicidal behaviors, such as giving away prized possessions, self-inflicted wounds, suicide notes, or words like, "I wish I could just die" are all indicators of destructive behavior patterns. If your teenager is showing any of these signs, take heed. Their feelings of loss and grief are no justification for destroying themselves. Your teenager is hurting and needs help. Pain and loss are realities of life, and your teenager needs to learn how to cope with them. Seek immediate guidance from an experienced grief counselor who can help your son or daughter through this difficult time.

Keep boundaries intact. Yes, death can change a lot of things in a teenager's life. But for their own growth and development, there must still be boundaries, or rules, to give them the direction and security they need. A death shouldn't change any family rules or boundaries that were in place before the death. Though your son or daughter may try to push their limits or manipulate you by using their sadness as an excuse for poor behavior, you can tell them, "I ain't buying it." Let them know that they are still responsible and accountable for their choices and actions. Use these opportunities to talk about the deeper issues of their pain and grief.

Enlist the support of friends, teachers, coaches, and counselors. If you feel every attempt you make to talk with your son or daughter is met with hostility, apathy, or resentment, you are not alone. Many parents of teenagers struggle to develop good communication with their children. When a death occurs, the volatile mix of confusing emotions makes communication even more difficult. Find someone you think your son or daughter respects, or at least someone with whom they would be willing to spend some time talking. Ask the person (a relative, family friend, youth minister, teacher, or coach) to call your child to go out for a Coke or to the movies. You may have to be a bit sneaky in your efforts as many young people resent a meeting contrived by their parents. Your role here is to provide the best available resources and people who will have a positive influence in the life of your teenager.

Develop an atmosphere of acceptance. It's important to remember that while you can't control your son's or daughter's emotions or behavior, you can develop an atmosphere of acceptance so that when your son or daughter is ready to talk, they can approach you safely. Be there to lend support if needed. As you deal with your own grief, be aware of your teenager's need for your attention and support.

Help create positive memories. Some teenagers will be plagued with guilt over what they did or didn't do, what they said or didn't say before the death occurred. While it's important not to minimize those feelings, it can also be helpful to focus on the things they did do right and the positive memories they do have of the person who died. Buy your son or daughter a journal. Have them write down their feelings, thoughts, and memories. If they have artistic talents, encourage them to draw a picture. They could also write poetry, compose a song, create a memory scrapbook filled with pictures, or write a note to the person who died.

Take It from PJ

If you're a teenager reading this book, here's some words of wisdom from someone who knows what it's like to lose a loved one. Take a few moments to think about what PJ says about working through your grief. Yeah, his experience is different from yours, but his ideas are definitely worth checking out.

- Don't bottle your emotions. Figure out what you're feeling and accept your feelings for what they are. Be totally honest.
- Share what you're feeling with a loved one, a friend, or someone who will listen.
- Lying does not help the grief you are feeling. Lying only makes the grief worse.
- Don't tell yourself, "I'll deal with it tomorrow." Deal with your grief now.
- Bad things are going to happen in life no matter what you believe.
- Let God know exactly what you're feeling. He can handle it.

Looking for more ideas? Creating meaningful memories helps the healing process.

10

Making Meaning, Making Memories

Celebrating Life with Children

When at a loss for words, create a ritual.
Anonymous

*T*he story of the boating accident and death of Joel Watt in chapter 1 would be incomplete if I didn't share with you what happened *after* Joel's death on the Sacramento River Delta. A few days before Joel's memorial service, the Watt family, Joel's girlfriend, Andrea, his best friend, Peter, and a number of family friends who were at the Delta when the accident occurred headed back to the Delta. An accident scene is the last place most people choose to revisit.

A couple days before his death, Joel began to ski the slalom course from behind the family's tournament ski boat. Anyone who has ever water-skied knows that attempting to maneuver around six buoys from behind a speeding boat on one ski is a considerable challenge. Only expert water-skiers need apply.

Cruising past the first buoy at thirty-five miles an hour, Joel successfully made it around the first three buoys on his first attempt. After each attempt on the slalom course, usually completed by a fantastic wipeout, Joel improved. With his arms growing tired from the tremendous strain of pulling against the rope to navigate each turn, Joel figured he had at least one more good run in him.

The boat accelerated with a growl, pulling Joel's large six-foot-five-inch frame out of the water. His water ski began to plane and Joel rose out of the murky Delta water. Setting up for the first of six pink buoys, Joel initiated his turn with a total sense of commitment and readiness to complete the course.

One buoy.

Two buoys.

Three buoys.

A chorus of screams cheering him on hollered out from the boat and from the shore, where a couple of people were watching. Until now, Joel had only completed four buoys. He still had three more to go in order to finish the whole course.

Racing for his next target, Joel leaned down toward the smooth, glassy water, stretched himself over the fourth pink buoy, and pulled the ski handle in hard toward his hip. Screaming across the foamy, bubbling boat wake, Joel cut into his next turn with all the eagerness of a one-year-old digging into his first birthday cake. Arms burning with fatigue, Joel stayed focused and sliced a smooth, high-arcing wall of water around the fifth buoy.

The fifth buoy!

Another enthusiastic set of screams roared from the boat and the shore. Joel had run the first five buoys so well, he was actually early for the last one. The sixth buoy was all his. The only thing he had to do was complete his final finishing turn. One more final cut around that bobbing pink ball and he was finished.

Joel couldn't believe what had just happened. In all the excitement and thrill of completing five buoys, Joel stood up. *Wrong move.* Crashing into the water with the grace of a train derailment, Joel submarined himself between the fifth and sixth buoys.

That sixth buoy had his name on it. That little bobbing ball, right there for the taking.

Hopping back into the boat, Joel was greeted with cheers reminiscent of those "thrill-of-victory-and-agony-of-defeat" groans found in every high-speed sport: "Great job, Joel! You were so close. You had it!"

Had he not stood up, Joel would have completed the course. Everyone in the boat knew he could have done it. *He was so close.* In his heart, Joel knew he could have made it too.

As a small flotilla of boats approached the slalom course a few days before Joel's memorial service, Joel's brothers, Jake and Jeremiah, mounted a jet-ski and slowly maneuvered through the slalom course. Carrying a flower wreath and Joel's ashes, Jake and Jeremiah turned around the sixth buoy, finishing the course Joel never completed. Jacob slipped into the water and laid a wreath on the sixth buoy. With that, the two brothers scattered Joel's ashes in the Delta water, a fitting symbol to a special life that had run its course.

A few thoughts and prayers were shared about Joel's life, his family and closest friends still in shock that he was no longer with them. Returning to the site of his last, perhaps most personal victory, Joel's family and friends created a sense of meaning out of this tragedy by symbolically completing the sixth buoy. The sixth buoy became a symbol of completion. A symbol of closure. And yes, a very real and lasting way to say good-bye to Joel in a place he loved so well. For Joel's family and friends, completing the sixth buoy was a gift to Joel. And a gift to themselves.

Memories for This Lifetime

Do you remember the words of Tom Hanks's son in the movie *Sleepless in Seattle*? As the two of them sit on a couch talking about the recent death of their wife and mother, the ten-year-old says in a soft voice, "I'm beginning to forget her."

Forgetting is a very real fear for every grieving person.

The following ideas are creative ways to help you and your children remember and celebrate the life of a loved one who has died. You can make meaning with your children by making memories. You can use many of these activities in a funeral or memorial service. Or you can do them with your children during special times of the year such as holidays and birthdays. Each one of these activities will present the opportunity to talk with your children about the life and death of the person who died. Not only are these activities special ways to remember a loved one, they are also important tools for helping children work through their feelings of grief.

Release a balloon. The only time children like seeing a balloon fly away is when they get to release it. Sending balloons into the sky is a very concrete way for children to send messages of love to someone who has died. Since many children think of heaven as being way, way up in the sky, releasing a balloon offers a fitting way of expressing feelings of longing and grief. A balloon release is a very relevant way for children to be involved in the grieving process, particularly at a funeral for a child. Have children write short notes and attach them to the balloon string. Balloon releases can be done on birthdays, holidays, and "anniversary of death" dates. If you have environmental concerns about a balloon release, another option is to rent a real hot-air balloon and go for a ride.

Plant a garden. Kids love to dig in the dirt. Planting a garden is not only a healthy activity, but it is also a meaningful metaphor for the seasons of life. Ask your children what kind of garden they'd like to plant—a flower garden, vegetable garden, or herb garden. Name the garden after the person who died. Make a colorful sign out of wood and paint the person's name on it.

Draw a picture. This activity appeals to most kids. Drawing and other forms of art are used extensively in grief therapy for children; these are simple ways for children to express what they're feeling about death. Draw pictures of home and ask your children about it. Have your kids select a topic to draw and see what they create. Use clay and have them create a scene that reminds them of the loved one who died.

Write a letter. Each year "Santa Claus" receives hundreds of thousands of letters in the mail addressed to the North Pole. Why not address a letter to heaven? Have your son or daughter write down everything they want to say, or everything they wished they could have said to the person who died. Address the letter to heaven and pop it in the mail. (It's better not to put your return address on this one!)

Create a tradition. Sit down with your children and brainstorm creative ideas to remember your loved one through a tradition that will be all your own. The birthday, anniversary of death, and favorite holiday of the deceased loved one are good times to develop traditions. Traditions could include a special memory service, a visit to the cemetery, an annual trip, or making a favorite meal. This can be especially meaningful to children as they create their own ways of making meaning out of death. The tradition you create may change over the years as your children grow, but that's okay. The important thing to remember is to make the tradition relevant for them.

Make a memorial. Particularly in the case of accidents, people will leave flowers, notes, candles, or photos at the accident scene. If it is in your best judgment to do this with your children (especially if they want to and if it is safe), create a memorial by asking for their ideas and involvement. Let your children know that this is a temporary memorial and it probably will be removed by a roadside cleaning crew. Don't leave anything your children expect to receive back. If this is not a good option, you can always make a memorial at home.

Light a candle. This is a simple yet symbolic way of remembering and reflecting on the life of a loved one. You can light a candle at your church, your home, at the grave site, or in some other special place.

Create a memory album. When Charlotte Dean died, friends and family whom Charlotte knew throughout all the stages of her life contributed stories, photos, and special memories for an album. This memory album was created for Josh and Sarah so they could have a very concrete reminder of their mother. You could do the same. Ask friends, family, coworkers, previous teachers, and classmates to send material for a memory album. It will create a beautiful collage of the person's life and personality.

Don't forget those "hand-me-downs." Children tend to get tired of hand-me-downs, but mementos from a loved one can be very important. A favorite watch, baseball, tie, book, ring, sweater. Small children may initially be indifferent about receiving a memento that belonged to a deceased parent or relative, but later in life an old watch or framed photograph may take on special meaning. Children who have lost a sibling may want to wear a favorite sweatshirt or hang on to some other favorite item of their brother or sister. This is normal "attachment" behavior a sibling will exhibit as a way to deal with their grief.

Make a quilt. Making a quilt for a loved one has become a popular way to remember someone who has died. The practice of making a memorial quilt has brought national attention to the need for more AIDS research.

Make the person's favorite meal. Todd Dean and his children did this activity with their family grief recovery group. Every family brought the deceased person's favorite meal for a potluck dinner. This is not only an easy way to involve children, but it is also a special way to remember the times this meal was shared by the whole family.

Write a poem or song. Writing a poem or song is a creative activity that appeals to older children and teenagers, particularly those who are creative or musically inclined. Personalized poems and songs are especially meaningful at funeral services. Make copies for everyone who attends the service.

Create a scholarship fund. Scholarship funds are very specific ways to help other young people who would not otherwise have the opportunity to go to college, camp, or some other activity. Get your children involved in deciding the purpose of the scholarship, selecting the scholarship applicants, and presenting the scholarship award. Scholarship or gift funds are often very useful for hospitals, research centers, and camps for underprivileged children.

Develop an organization. Sound a bit overwhelming? Most children will not start an organization, but many organizations have developed as a result of tragedy. Take M.A.D.D., Mothers Against Drunk Driving, for example. There is no limit to the creative power of individuals who vow to right the wrongs in our society.

Make a videotape. Go through that old stack of videos sitting on the family room shelf and find footage of the person who died. If you have a teenager with technical and photographic skills, this is a unique way for him or her to create a meaningful memory. Even if working with a video isn't a strength for you alone, this just may be a project your family can tackle together.

Go on the person's favorite vacation. Like making a favorite meal, try taking a vacation to the deceased person's favorite place. The best thing to do, as you think about your needs as well as your children's, is to think about how this vacation will be significant for everyone involved.

Visit the grave site. A cemetery can be visited again and again. Taking your children to visit a loved one's grave can open a flood of questions and memories related to the funeral service. In the case of small children who did not participate in the funeral, you will want to prepare them with what a cemetery looks like and what you'll do while you're there.

Buy a locket. Your daughter may cherish a simple gold locket with a picture of her mother, father, brother, sister, grandparent, or friend. You don't have to spend a lot of money to buy a piece of "memory jewelry." For a boy, you may want to buy a watch, engraved ring, or gold chain.

Dedicate a library bookshelf. This idea is particularly meaningful when a child or classmate dies. Go to your local library or the library at your son or daughter's school and ask for a bookshelf to be dedicated in the child's name. Ask friends, family, and families of classmates to donate a book for the bookshelf. Have a nameplate engraved and placed on the shelf. You may even want to purchase some small reading chairs or beanbag chairs to be placed near the bookshelf.

Make a slide show. When Joel Watt died, his father poured a lot of energy into creating a wonderful slide show for Joel's memorial service. Even in the midst of many tears, the slide presentation set off bursts of much-needed laughter as funny slides of Joel came across the screen. Joel made a lot of people laugh; a thoughtful slide show will present accurate snapshots of the person's personality. With music dubbed in, a slide show can capture deep feelings and emotions, making words no longer necessary.

Talk about your loved one. It sounds so simple, doesn't it? Talking about a loved one who has died can bring them back to life in word pictures and stories. This can be particularly important with young children who don't have a memory of their deceased parent. By talking about your loved one, you can create a tangible personal picture of the person who died. From time to time, my wife and I talk about our friend, Dana, who died seven years ago from cancer. Recalling his laughter, his smile, and all the fun memories of him help us laugh and remember the joy of his friendship. Mixed with our laughter is also the pain of our loss. To not remember Dana would be more painful than the pleasure of his memory.

Why Making Meaning Makes Sense

About a century ago, a man by the name of Horatio Spafford stood at the bow of a slow, gently rolling ship on the high seas off the coast of England. As he looked out at the expansive, rolling sea before him, Horatio Spafford reached deep into an unseen reservoir of faith and penned a tender, moving song of tribute that would influence millions of lives in the coming century.

Only days earlier, Spafford had stood on the docks in America waving good-bye to his wife and four daughters who had just boarded the *Ville du Havre*, a ship bound for Europe. After attending to a few business matters, Spafford had planned to meet his wife and daughters in Europe for a family vacation. His hopes for a family vacation turned into a family tragedy. During the voyage, the *Ville du Havre* collided with another ship, the *Lochearn*, and sank. Mrs. Spafford survived the accident, but all four daughters perished.

When news arrived of the accident, Horatio Spafford took the next boat across the Atlantic to be reunited with his wife in Cardiff, Wales. While sailing past the spot where his daughters drowned, he wrote the moving words to the classic hymn, "It Is Well with My Soul."[8]

> When peace like a river attendeth my way,
> When sorrows like sea billows roll,
> Whatever my lot, you have taught me to say,
> It is well, it is well with my soul.
>
> It is well . . . with my soul.
> It is well, it is well with my soul.

All death is loss. And whether a death is accidental or expected, as is often the case with terminal illnesses and elderly people, our souls may ring empty with the hollow echo of senselessness. It's not enough to justify to ourselves and others, "Well, at least my grandfather lived a long and full life." We can't minimize the impact of a person's absence or deny the influence they had in our lives.

In death, our soul cries out for meaning. We want so desperately to keep the life and memory of our loved ones alive. In families where there is unresolved conflict and a history of pain, death can accentuate the strained, even abusive relationships. We need meaning and a definite sense of significance to offset the weight of grief and the burden of tragedy. Making meaning helps us make sense of the tragedy of death.

At first glance, some people might classify Horatio Spafford as a simple-minded, religious fool for writing a song of faith after the death of his four daughters. Critics might say, "A braver man would accept his fate without leaning on the crutch of faith." Yes, some people cringe at the mention of making meaning out of what appears to be utterly meaningless. What meaning is there in tragedy? What meaning is there in a senseless, unnecessary death? The idea of making meaning out of such a loss can seem wholly insensitive and inappropriate. The search for meaning in death can easily lead the bereaved person down the well-trodden, question-strewn path of "why."

Questions rage inside us when we cannot explain the unexplainable. As I mentioned in the introduction, the purpose of this book is not to answer the "why" questions. I cannot even begin to speak for the Almighty or for you and the grief you may be experiencing. I also do not want to be guilty of being like one of Job's counselors, who offered foolish, insensitive explanations for his loss.

For a grieving person, the fact that "God moves in mysterious ways" isn't good enough.

Ask any grieving person their thoughts about the truly clueless individuals who attempt to explain why their daughter died in a car accident, or why a newborn baby only lived for a few short days, or why their father died of a sudden heart attack, or why God acts in such mysterious ways, and you'll hear visceral, almost vindictive responses from the grieving person wanting to knock that person into next week. And rightly so.

For a grieving person, the fact that "God moves in mysterious ways" isn't good enough. Would God really be God if he wasn't somewhat mysterious? Would God really be God if we could know everything about him? Of course God moves in mysterious ways, but who are we to speak for him and the mystery of his nature? No person, no matter how well-meaning or how misguided, has the right, much less the invitation, to answer the "why" question for another. It is a holy, sacred question between the grieving person and God. It is a question, in more cases than not, in which God chooses to be silent. The question "why" is a profound three letter word which humans all too frequently botch at the expense and pain of the grieving person. There is wisdom in silence. There is also wisdom in making meaning when life doesn't make sense.

My objective is to move some of us closer to meaning. Every death is marked with someone's deep sense of personal loss and pain. Every death, in one way or another, has the "why" question attached to it. While asking "why" can be a sincere question of faith, it is also a question that can leave a distinct and hopeless void in our soul. Where there is the absence of meaning, we can be suffocated with the oppressiveness of the question. The alternative to living with such a void is to create meaning by remembering our loved ones in healthy, creative ways.

Making meaning makes sense because it helps us to grieve the loss of a loved one in positive, nondestructive ways. Remembering the fond moments, unique personality traits, special talents and skills, physical features, character strengths and quirks, likes and dislikes, interests and hobbies is an important and critical task in helping us deal with the immensity of our loss and pain. As I interviewed family after family for this book, the most chilling words I heard came from the voice of Doug Watt, who said, "The thing that hurts the most is when people don't acknowledge that you even had a son."

For anyone who has experienced the death of a loved one, remembering is life. It is far more painful to try to forget. For everyone else, forgetting is all too easy. That's why making meaning out of the person's life is such an important task.

In sorting through the messy process of grief, we ultimately arrive at a choice of hope or despair. Meaning moves us toward hope. Though the pain of losing a loved one never goes away, its intensity lessens over time as we redefine, reevaluate, and reinvest in the life we still have to live. *If we choose hope.* To choose otherwise is to live with a sense of resigned indifference to a chaotic fate we have no control over.

> *We don't have to be people of great faith in order to be people of faith.*

In all of this, there are still choices to make. *Hard, difficult choices.* We can choose despair. Or we can choose to make meaning. We can choose to be people of hope. We can choose to model a living, yet broken faith in God. We can be weak in our pain and, yes, even unsure in our hope. As best we can, we can pass on to our children the message of hope and life in Jesus Christ. The wonderful beauty of the gospel is that God's message of acceptance, love, and hope is not dependent on our performance, our questions, our faith, our strength, or our lack thereof. The hope of his message transcends our pain. The meaning of his love remains the same to the very depths of our soul.

The picture of Horatio Spafford leaning against a cold railing and writing a meaningful song of faith as his ship passed the place where his daughters perished touches a part of our soul most of us don't even realize exists. There is a deep part of us that longs to live by faith. We long for a sense of meaning and significance in this life. However, we don't have to be people of *great* faith in order to be people of faith. We don't have to write classic hymns in order to make meaning out of death. As I'm sure Horatio Spafford would say, in your own way—even when the tragedy of death doesn't make sense—you can say in faith, "Whatever my lot, you have taught me to say, it is well with my soul." And even if the loss of a loved one is not well with your soul, that's okay too. God understands.

Understanding how to help your children, yourself, and others is an important step in healing your broken soul.

11

What Can I Do?

Helping Children, Loved Ones, and Yourself in the Grieving Process

The friend who can be silent with us in a moment of despair or confusion . . . who can stay with us in an hour of grief and bereavement . . . who can tolerate not caring, not healing, and face with us the reality of our powerlessness . . . that is a friend who cares.

Henri Nouwen

This is the most important chapter in this book. I sincerely hope you've made it this far. Or maybe, just maybe, you've flipped right to this chapter first. A good idea, especially if you're wondering how to help yourself, your children, or others who may be hurting from the death of a loved one.

One of the difficult discoveries I made as I interviewed families for this book was the reality of how many grieving people get hurt by people who sincerely want to help. Without thinking, some people innocently say the wrong thing on the phone or at a funeral service. After a death occurs, there are always those individuals who *say* they want to help but never get in and actually do the helping. And yes, there are always those rare, mean-spirited individuals who hurt to hurt. I recall reading one Internet grief newsgroup in which one woman whose daughter had died recounted what her mother had said: "Oh, honey, I know *just* how you feel. I felt the same way when my horse died."

Some people. Fortunately, by the time you finish reading this chapter, you are going to have a better awareness of how to take care of yourself, your children, and those around you who may be grieving. This chapter is loaded with great ideas, quotes, poems, and insights from people who have shared the grief experience. Use this material to better understand the needs of your children, those you love, and even yourself. Put to good use the wisdom found here from those who have journeyed the path of grief ahead of you. It will help you make a positive difference in others' lives, both now and for all eternity.

Understanding the Components of Grief

Grief is a very confusing experience for both the bereaved and those who try to comfort them. Since every death is unique and every person's experience of grief is unique, it is impossible to completely understand what the bereaved person is going through. A child who has lost a mother will have a different grief experience than the husband who lost a wife. A grandparent who lost a grandchild will grieve differently than the mother and father who lost the child. Children who lose a sibling will grieve differently than their parents. Friends and relatives who share in the family's loss will also have a different grief experience. Throw in all the different issues we have discussed in this book—such as family dynamics, finances, dealing with friends at school, fears about the future, questions of faith, and so on—and we can see how grief is a tremendously difficult experience.

Grieving people are frequently misunderstood. It is not uncommon to hear someone make an under-the-breath comment like, "It's been eight months now. Can't they just get over it?" Grieving people don't "get over it." They learn to live through their grief. Along the way, a grieving person undergoes intense physical, emotional, mental, and spiritual challenges.

Understanding the various components, characteristics, and attributes of grief can help you to be sensitive to another's grief. It can also help you to identify and understand the characteristics of your own grief. Cendra Lynn, Ph.D, is the moderator of the Internet grief support group called "Griefnet" (http://www.rivendell.org). As an expert in bereavement issues, Dr. Lynn has outlined the various components of grief.[9] This information can greatly aid all of us who wish to cope with grief in healthy, constructive ways. By better understanding the complexity of grief, we can hopefully become more sensitive and compassionate to those who are hurting.

Behavioral Components of Grief

Restlessness
Compulsiveness
Social withdrawal
Hyperactivity
Lassitude
Increased interaction
Escape into work
Overprotectiveness
Experiencing presence
  of deceased
Apathy

Angry outbursts
Clinging to loved ones
Change in relationship to
  family
Change in relationship to
  partner
Change in relationship to
  friends
Incorporation of deceased's
  behaviors

Emotional Components of Grief

Anger	Blaming
Desolation	Longing for deceased
Hopelessness	Despair
Panic	Anxiety
Guilt	Fear
Denial	Relief
Idealization	Sadness
Shame	Jealousy

Mental Components of Grief

Preoccupation with thoughts of deceased	Analyzing
	Active avoidance of the topic
Reliving the loss	Incorporation of deceased's ways of thinking
Obsessing	
Rationalizing	Continuation of deceased's work
Intellectualizing	

Physical Components of Grief

Immediate Responses

Chills	Change in heart rate
Weakness	Vision changes
Difficulty breathing	Numbness
Nausea	Changes in hearing
Change in blood pressure	Sleep disorders
Anorexia	Death

Minor Physical Responses

Colds	Minor injuries
Flu	Aches and pains
Minor asthma attacks	Restlessness

Major Physical Responses

Pneumonia	Anxiety disorder
Heart attack	Phobias
Substance abuse	Depression
Cancer	Death

Chronic Physical Responses

Arthritis	Series of accidents
Skin disorders	Sleep disorders
Hypertension	Depression

Spiritual Components of Grief

Loss/increase of faith

Distancing from/increased activity with clergy, rituals

Preoccupation with the meaning of life/death

Need to turn this experience into something meaningful

Existentialism

Awareness of life's fragility

Morbidness

Productiveness

Increased/decreased intimacy with others

Experiencing presence of deceased—seeing, hearing, smelling, feeling

How to Help the Hurting

You want to help someone who has lost a loved one. It may be a friend, a coworker, a neighbor, or a relative, but you are terribly afraid of saying or doing something wrong. If you're anything like me, you don't want to do something stupid. Don't worry . . . you're not alone. You can be a comfort and support to a grieving person by simply being with them. You can offer the gift of your presence.

In helping a grieving person, your words will probably be forgotten. Your deeds might be remembered. But it is your presence that will stick in their hearts and minds forever. Presence is what people remember most.

> *You can be a comfort and support to a grieving person by simply being with them. You can offer the gift of your presence.*

One of my favorite authors, Henri Nouwen, warns us to never underestimate the power of presence. Your presence alone has a tremendous and powerful effect on sharing the loss others are feeling. Nouwen writes:

> We say, "Why should I visit this person? I can't do anything for anyone. I don't even have anything to say. Of what use can I be?" Meanwhile, we have forgotten that it is often in "useless," unpretentious, humble presence to each other that we feel consolation and comfort. Simply being with someone is difficult because it asks of us that we share in the other's vulnerability, enter with him or her into the experience of weakness and powerlessness, become part of uncertainty, and give

up control and self-determination. And still, whenever this happens, new strength and new hope is being born.[10]

Next, along with the power of your presence, listening is a specific way to help a grieving person who is trying to process the spinning tornado of emotions blowing inside. Listening is a wonderful gift, but how few there are who lavish it upon others. You can help your children, your spouse, your parents, your friends, or your neighbor simply by your willingness to listen to what's on their heart. When a grieving person feels safe from the warmth of another person's presence, it doesn't take much to get them to open up. Listening doesn't involve giving advice, offering solutions, seeking details, explaining the unexplainable, or taking charge of the situation. Listening means simply listening. We all know what it is. We all know how much better we feel when someone listens to us. We'd all like others to say about us, "That person is such a good listener." Are you listening?

The following selection by Debbie Gemmill captures the essence of a grieving person's desire not just to be heard, but to be actually listened to.

Could You Please Just Listen?

My baby has died. Please don't tell me you know how I feel. You don't. You can't. I hope you never do.

Don't tell me he's with God and I should be happy. How can I be happy when every time I go into his nursery all I see is an empty crib and toys that will never be played with? How can I be happy when my arms ache to hold him?

Please don't tell me God needed another angel. It's hard for me to understand why God would take away this little one who was so loved. Maybe I'll understand later. But for right now . . . let God find another angel.

Please, please, please don't tell me I'll have other children. Maybe I will . . . but my son was not a puppy that ran away. He cannot be replaced.

Maybe you could just listen when I remember out loud all the things we did together—the walks, the early morning feedings, the first time he rolled over. Maybe you could just sit with me while I cry over all the things we'll never do together.

Please don't tell me it could be worse. How?

I really don't want to hear about your grandfather's death. It's not the same. Don't think my pain will be eased by comparison. Of course I'm glad that he didn't suffer, but I'd be a lot happier if he hadn't died at all.

I know it must be hard for you, but would you mind looking at his picture just one more time? We don't have many of him, and I'm just a little bit afraid that I may forget what he looked like. He wasn't here that long, you know.

Could you please just listen?

Don't tell me I'll get over it. There is no "over it," only *through* it. Maybe you could just be with me while I take my first steps through it.

Please don't tell me I should be glad he was just a baby, or that at least I did get to know him. I knew him. I knew him before I ever saw him. He is a part of me. And now he is gone. I haven't just lost a seven-month-old baby. I have lost a part of myself.

I know you mean well, but please don't expect me to tell you how to help me. I'd tell you if I knew, but right now I can hardly put one foot in front of the other. Maybe if you looked around, you could find some things to do, like taking my daughter for a walk, or doing the dishes, or making some coffee.

Please don't try to remove my pain or distract me from it. I have to feel this way right now.

Maybe you could just listen.[11]

Should I Take the Kids to the Funeral?

If you're wondering whether or not to take your kids to the funeral of a loved one, then you're asking one of the most common questions about kids and funerals. Many parents wonder if taking a child to a funeral service or graveside memorial will harm their children in any way. That's a legitimate question. The answer is, "It depends." As you can imagine, I lean toward including children in the funeral process and the family faith tradition because it presents a perfect opportunity to talk to children about the reality of life and death. However, there are specific situations in which parents must use wisdom and caution in considering what is in their children's best interest. For example, if a child is physically incapacitated due to the emotional shock of the death, or if the child expresses strong fears or objections about attending the funeral, he or she should not be forced to attend.

In general, children should not be made to go to funerals, but instead, they should be provided as much information in advance about what happens at funerals in order to allay their fears. With proper education and preparation, parents can help their children have a meaningful funeral experience. In many cases, children can be active participants in a funeral service by reading a poem or Scripture, carrying flowers, singing a song, or telling a story. Whether or not you decide to take your children to the funeral of a loved one, here are some helpful ideas to consider.

- Allow your children to participate in the funeral service.
- Ask yourself, "How will my children feel if they are not allowed to attend?"
- Think about the schedule of the funeral and how that will affect young children.
- For toddlers and very small children, bring snacks, juice, crayons, and books to keep them occupied during a long service.
- Be sure to keep your children close by you throughout the day.
- If a child wants to attend the funeral, talk about what will happen before the event occurs.

- Talk with your children about their feelings of grief and loss.
- Ask your children questions about what they saw and experienced at the funeral.
- Be aware of what others may say to your child about the deceased.
- Be sure to explain new ideas and terms that may confuse children (i.e., grave, cremation, hearse, etc.).
- Be aware of people who may try to distract your children from the grief experience by offers of candy, toys, sleepovers, etc.

Warning Signs

Suffering the loss of a loved one and entering the grieving process is one of the most painful and difficult challenges a person can ever face. It is important to be aware of the warning signs of potentially harmful behaviors. If you, your children, or someone you know is experiencing any of these warning signs, you may want to consult a professional counselor, minister, or health professional.

- Protracted inability to believe that your loved one has really died.
- Long-term social isolation following the death.
- Inability to care for yourself.
- Inability to care for children.
- Dependence upon alcohol or drugs to mask pain, relieve anguish, loneliness, anger, guilt, sadness, or other grief-related emotions.
- Great effort to *avoid* thinking of the loved one who died.
- Significant weight gain, weight loss, panic attacks, insomnia, chronic depression, or a marked deterioration of health.

- Suicidal thoughts, words, or gestures, or even an attempted suicide.
- Prolonged inability to "get on" with life, to invest energy in living.[12]

Though you may experience one or more of these warning signs during the grieving process, talking with a professional counselor or a trusted friend can help you deal with your grief in a healthy way.

Ideas, Ideas, and More Ideas

There are so many simple and practical ways to help a grieving family or individual. Loretta Ricciardi, The Compassionate Friends (a nationwide organization dedicated to helping mothers and fathers who have experienced the death of a child),[13] and the many families I interviewed have graciously contributed the following ideas and insights.

Bereaved parents often say things like, "I wish my child hadn't died," or "I wish I had him back." Another wish is, "I wish my friends, or church, or neighbors, or relatives understood about the loss of our child." Here is a partial list of such wishes.[14]

When You Wish upon a Star

1. I wish you would not be afraid to speak my child's name. My child lived and was important and I need to hear his name.
2. If I cry or get emotional when we talk about my child, I wish you knew that it isn't because you have hurt me; the fact that my child died has caused my tears. You have allowed me to cry and I thank you. Crying and emotional outbursts are healing.
3. I wish you wouldn't "kill" my child again by removing from your home his pictures, artwork, or other remembrances.

4. I will have emotional highs and lows, ups and downs. I wish you wouldn't think that if I have a good day my grief is all over, or that if I have a bad day I need psychiatric counseling.
5. I wish you knew that the death of a child is different from other losses and the hurt should be viewed separately. It is the ultimate tragedy, and I wish you wouldn't compare it to your loss of a parent, a spouse, or a pet.
6. Being a bereaved parent is not contagious, so I wish you wouldn't stay away from me.
7. I wish you knew all of the "crazy" grief reactions that I am having are in fact very normal. Depression, anger, frustration, hopelessness, and the questioning of values and beliefs are to be expected following the death of a child.
8. I wish you wouldn't expect my grief to be over in six months. The first few years are going to be exceedingly traumatic for us. As with alcoholics, I will never be "cured" or a "former bereaved parent," but will forevermore be a recovering bereaved parent.
9. I wish you understood the physical reactions to grief. I may gain weight or lose weight, sleep all the time or not at all, develop a host of illnesses, and be accident-prone.
10. I wish you knew that our child's birthday, the anniversary of his death, and holidays are terrible times.

Do's and Don'ts for Helping Grieving Persons

Do...

Help with meals and major chores. Many grieving people don't feel like leaving their home, so volunteering to assist with chores such as running errands and baby-sitting can be a big help.

Communicate your availability through action. It is helpful when people communicate that they are available for anything—and then put their availability into action. Don't ignore a grieving person because you don't feel comfortable and don't know what to say. Your presence is more important than your words. Keep in touch with them and offer your support.

Pick up the phone. A simple, short conversation on the telephone shows your care and concern for the grieving person. If the death has just occurred, make listening a priority and keep your words few.

Talk about the deceased person. If you knew the deceased person, talk about him or her. Don't be afraid to mention his or her name. Tell the family how much you loved their child and that you think about the child often. Let the family know the child is still alive in your heart and mind. It is a tremendous help to the family to let them know you loved this person and are sharing in their grief.

Hug and hug some more. Touching is healing!

Contact close friends or family members. Especially in the case of sudden, accidental deaths, it may be helpful to contact someone close to the family such as a cousin, aunt, uncle, or close family friend instead of calling the immediate family.

Send a card. From time to time, especially at holidays or on the child's birthday, send a card to let the person know you are thinking about them. Don't forget to send personal letters to the children as well. Kids love to receive mail! Share with the family your favorite memories of the person who died and let them know how the person's life has affected yours.

Use God's Word responsibly. Yes, God's Word can be a source of great comfort and encouragement in times of suffering. But the loss of a loved one can be a very difficult spiritual experience as the grieving person wrestles with God and the question of why the death occurred. Even for someone who has a very strong faith, the last thing they may want to hear are verses about victory over death, resurrection, or heaven. Some people of faith may take great encouragement from God's Word in their time of need; others may not. Use great wisdom and caution here.

Let your words be few. In interviewing the many families who contributed to this book, the overwhelming response of the words that meant the most to them were the simple, heartfelt words, "I'm so sorry."

Buy a book. Books, especially grieving and bereavement literature, can be useful tools for the times when a grieving person is alone. There are many excellent resources available for children, teenagers, and adults designed to help individuals understand the grieving process. Grieving individuals usually prefer to learn from professionals who understand the grieving process; personal stories written from another person who has lost a loved one are also helpful. However, if you see a pile of "grief books" on the kitchen counter, make a batch of chocolate chip cookies instead.

Remember birthdays, anniversaries, and holidays. Christmas. Hanukkah. Easter. Halloween. Memorial Day. Thanksgiving. Valentine's Day. Wedding anniversaries. Birthdays. Mother's Day. Father's Day. The beginning and end of the school year. Christmas and summer vacations. These special days and times throughout the year are marked by the loved one's absence. In homes where a parent has died, offer to help out with the children's birthdays. Send flowers or a card on the deceased person's birthday and on the anniversary of the death. Don't expect that the family should be excited or happy during the holidays. Tell them you know it's a hard time for them and that you are praying for them. Tell them you are also thinking of their loved one who has died. By remembering these important dates, you will keep the very special memory of the loved one alive.

Don't...

Pressure. Don't push a grieving person to do anything be-fore they are ready, whether it be going out to social events or putting away the child's belongings. Let them take their time in putting their life back in order, and be there to support them when they are.

Rationalize. Avoid offering reasons for why the loved one has died. Saying, "It was a blessing," or, "They're in a better place," does not make the family feel any better. A simple and heartfelt "I'm sorry" is what they need to hear. When a parent or child is grieving, there is no reason or explanation that is going to make them feel better. They don't want the death justified or explained by you. All they want is your understanding and compassion.

Try to cheer them up. A grieving person doesn't want to be cheered up right now; they want to grieve. It's insensitive to try to pretend that they aren't hurting and that they *should* be happy just because you want them to be.

Say, "You're so strong, you'll get through this." To the grieving person, it sounds like, "It's going to be easy for you to get through this because you didn't love your child that much." Losing a child is the worst thing anyone could go through. It is no easier for a "strong" person than it is for anyone else.

Say, "I don't know how you do it! If that happened to me, I would just die." First of all, the grieving person probably *wants* to die, so don't assume they are not dying inside, regardless of how they look on the outside. Second, they really don't have a choice of whether or not to wake up each day and face life, so don't make it sound like it is easy for them. And finally, *you* didn't lose your child, so please don't compare yourself to them because you really have no idea what it feels like.

Try to distract them from their grief. If you invite them out for an evening, don't try to distract them by taking them to a big, noisy party or a loud concert. Dinner at a nice quiet restaurant or a walk in the fresh air are more likely to be appealing choices. Casual conversation about sports, the news, or the weather is probably not what they are interested in. What is more meaningful is someone who will listen and share in their grief.

Last Words

We began this book walking through the shadowlands. As I've tried to convey—often very feebly, I'm afraid—death is not the end of the story. I believe with all my heart that heaven's not a crying place, and I look forward to the day when God will wipe away every tear from our eyes. Grief will be gone. There will be no more death. No more mourning. No more crying. No more pain.

The shadowlands will disappear in the light of God's brilliance.

This is our faith. This is our hope.

This is the wonderful gift we can give to our children.

In the first chapter, I shared with you a picture of the shadowlands—that of C. S. Lewis sobbing in the attic, embracing his stepson, David, both of them broken over the loss of a wife and mother. As you talk with your children about all their questions of death, dying, and eternal life, I hope you will embrace and hug them. I hope you courageously confront the fears that may keep you from telling your children as much as you know about life and death. As I've mentioned earlier, even though we may sometimes think we know a lot of things, there are still a lot of things we just can't know. We don't know the whole story, but we can know the Author of the story. That's a wonderful secret to let your kids in on. We don't know the whole story . . . *yet.* There's still a wonderful story waiting to be told.

Just as we can open the Bible and flip to the final pages of the Book of Revelation to get a glimpse of some of the wonders that await us in heaven, I offer you C. S. Lewis's final words in The Chronicles of Narnia as a fitting reminder that heaven's not a crying place.

"You do not yet look so happy as I mean you to be."

Lucy said, "We're so afraid of being sent away, Aslan. And you have sent us back into our own world so often."

"No fear of that," said Aslan. "Have you not guessed?"

Their hearts leaped and a wild hope rose within them.

"There *was* a real railway accident," said Aslan softly. "Your father and mother and all of you are—as you used to call it in the Shadow-Lands—dead. The term is over: the holidays have begun. The dream is ended: this is the morning."

And as He spoke He no longer looked to them like a lion; but the things that began to happen after that were so great and beautiful that I cannot write them. And for us this is the end of all the stories, and we can most truly say that they all lived happily ever after. But for them it was only the beginning of the real story. All their life in this world and all their adventures in Narnia had only been the cover and the title page: now at last they were beginning Chapter One of the Great Story, which no one on earth has read: which goes on for ever: in which every chapter is better than the one before.[15]

Appendix A

Questions and Answers about the Funeral Process

We live in a nation of planners. We eagerly plan for the birth of children. We plan for birthdays, holidays, and vacations. We plan for our careers by going to college or trade school. We plan for job advancements by attending graduate school or moving across the country. We begin our mornings by planning our top priorities of the day and scheduling our appointments.

Though we are a nation of planners, we are also a nation of procrastinators. Nowhere is this reality greater seen than in the average person's understanding of how the funeral process works. Funeral planning ranks right up there with surgery, taxes, and dieting as one of the "least favorite things to do" for Americans. Ask anyone who has had the responsibility of taking care of all the details involved in making funeral arrangements and you'll hear responses like this:

> "I had no idea there was so much involved in making funeral arrangements."
> "I didn't know I would have so many decisions to make."
> "Nobody ever told me there were so many options."
> "There were costs and fees and terms I didn't understand."

"I was so distraught . . . I didn't know what I wanted or what was best."

"My husband and I never talked about what he wanted in a funeral. When he died so suddenly, there was so little time to make so many decisions."

"I wish somebody would have explained all of this ahead of time."

"I wish I had been better prepared."

Like talking with your children about death and dying, understanding how to make funeral arrangements doesn't have to be an intimidating or mysterious process. By preparing and educating yourself about how the funeral process works in advance, you'll be better equipped to make decisions during the difficult time following a death. Best of all, by gaining the knowledge and understanding of how funeral arrangements work, you can be in a better position to be attentive to your children's needs and emotions. You'll definitely be better prepared to answer their inevitable questions.

By understanding some of the basic components of how funeral arrangements are made, you'll develop a clearer personal understanding of what you want and don't want, what you need and don't need in the many services offered by mortuaries. Also, as a consumer, you'll be able to ask intelligent questions about prices and fees for services. You will know what questions to ask a funeral director and how to find the quality of service you are looking for in a mortuary. By knowing what you want and need in arranging a funeral, you can save thousands of dollars by avoiding last-minute decisions driven by emotion and uncertainty.

A funeral service is a unique opportunity to celebrate the life of the deceased. It is a time to allow the living the opportunity to enter the necessary, painful process of mourning. Whether the funeral is a large, orchestrated affair with special music, eulogies, and personal testimonials, a traditional Catholic burial with a rosary and mass, a quiet grave-side service, or a direct cremation with a simple reception at the family's home, each funeral is an important time for family, friends, coworkers, and acquaintances to support one another. Whether the arrangements are being made for a parent, grandparent, spouse, child, or friend, every death is unique and so are the details for planning every funeral.

During the funeral arrangement process, a family will be asked dozens and dozens of questions. There is a vast range of options for what type of service a family would like from the mortuary. It is not unusual for a family to be asked *hundreds* of questions concerning their wishes and desires. Neil O'Connor, a director at O'Connor Laguna Hills Mortuary, states, "A family needs to discuss what they want in funeral arrangements before they ever step foot in a mortuary. The options are almost limitless. Families who are prepared can save themselves a lot of time and energy. Families who aren't prepared for answering so many questions and exploring their options can find the funeral arrangement process very difficult. That's why we like to stress funeral arrangement education long before a death in the family occurs."

The following material will help you to understand how the funeral process works. By the time you finish reading it, you will have a basic understanding of the decisions you will be asked to make. Once those decisions are made, you can move on to the more important matters of coming to terms with your own grief, spending time with your family, and attending to the needs of your children.

Selecting a Mortuary

Depending on the size of your town or city, your choices in selecting a mortuary may be limited. If you live in a large city, you will be able to choose from ten to fifteen mortuaries, cemeteries, and memorial societies. You may choose a cemetery that offers complete funeral arrangement services, a mortuary that does not operate a cemetery but uses several cemeteries for its clientele, or a cremation society that only offers direct cremation services. In smaller towns and cities, your options will be more limited, but there should be at least two to three mortuaries to choose from. If the town you live in does not have a mortuary, it will be important to find out what your options are in the adjoining cities. In selecting a mortuary, there are a number of important items to consider.

Ethnicity

Especially in large cities, some mortuaries may serve the particular needs and customs of specific races or ethnic groups better than others. The benefit of selecting a mortuary that serves a particular ethnic group is its understanding of that group's particular rites, rituals, and customs. Whether your heritage is Asian, African-American, Hispanic, American Indian, or Caucasian, your decision to choose a particular mortuary may be based, in part, on your ethnicity. Also, depending on where you live in a large city, location may be a consideration for those who will be attending the funeral service. Mortuaries that serve particular ethnic groups for the majority of their business are often located in specific ethnic neighborhoods.

Religious Affiliation

Closely related to the question of ethnicity is the religious affiliation of certain mortuaries. Some mortuaries, particularly those in large ethnic populations, are appealing to their clientele because of a certain religious affiliation. Though many mortuaries are owned by larger corporations, a specific religious affiliation may be a local specialty. While mortuaries cannot discriminate based upon someone's religious tradition, many mortuaries wind up serving certain religious traditions more than others. Jewish families often choose a Jewish mortuary. Catholic families will often choose a Catholic mortuary. Families of the various Protestant traditions will select a mortuary that serves their particular tradition. While practically all mortuaries will gladly serve a family regardless of their religious background, your decision to choose a mortuary may be based upon your religious affiliation.

Reputation and Customer Service

Like any other business or company you would choose to buy a product or service from, select a mortuary that has a positive reputation in your local community. You want to choose a mortuary that offers a high degree of quality service. Handling all the details of a funeral can be a very stressful process and you do not want to choose a mortuary whose staff is unwilling to listen patiently to your questions. The last thing you need is someone who will push you into making decisions you don't want to make. A mortuary with high-quality customer service provides all the time, information, and knowledge you need to make a good decision.

One of the best ways to evaluate the quality of a mortuary's customer service is simply to call and see if they will answer your questions on the telephone or not. Mortuaries with quality customer service know the value of taking care of people. Ask the mortuary to mail you information so you can become informed about their prices and range of services. Once you receive the information, evaluate it on its usefulness, clarity, and readability. When you are ready, make an appointment to meet with a staff member who will answer your questions and explain the funeral process without requiring you to sign or pay for anything. Before you select a mortuary, you want to be a knowledgeable buyer. Though most people don't like to think of selecting a mortuary as they would for any other product or service, remember this: You are still the customer.

Atmosphere

Perhaps you've driven past a certain mortuary for years but have never been inside the building. Your decision to choose a particular mortuary may be based solely on aesthetic reasons. A quality mortuary, like any other company or business, will be clean and well-maintained with a warm, people-oriented atmosphere. Comfortable furniture, quiet, relaxing music, informative literature, and fresh flowers are a good sign of a mortuary's attention to detail.

Price

If you live in a town that has a number of mortuaries, you have the benefit of not only evaluating each mortuary on its reputation, quality of service, and atmosphere but also on price. People unprepared to make funeral arrangements can become overwhelmed with the numerous merchandise choices, state-mandatory fees, and funeral costs. The average traditional funeral costs between thirty-five hundred dollars and fifty-five hundred dollars, so you want to be sure exactly what you want and don't want in a funeral service. You can avoid making sudden, emotional decisions by being informed which costs are mandatory and which are optional.

One of the most common scenarios related to price is when a husband and wife have not discussed their preferences for what they want or don't want in a funeral. A husband may simply want to be cremated, while his wife may want a large, lavish funeral affair. When a spouse dies, it is not uncommon for the surviving spouse to spend thousands of dollars on a beautiful casket that he or she thinks their spouse would have liked. The simplest way to make a good financial decision regarding funerals is to know exactly what your loved one's desire is for their funeral.

Generally, funerals for children are less expensive than funerals for adults. In some cases, such as infant deaths, mortuaries might graciously eliminate a number of costs and fees. If your family is experiencing financial hardship, find a mortuary that is not only affordable but may also offer some form of financial assistance through discounted prices or fees. Every business needs to make a profit, but there are many mortuaries that have developed fine reputations in showing compassion, putting the needs of people before profit.

Understanding Services, Facilities, and Equipment

When you call a number of mortuaries to receive their service and pricing information, you'll discover what types of services and options are available for your family. Though each mortuary will offer a variety of services, there are a number of general services and expenses you can expect to find in every mortuary. The following list explains the various services available at most mortuaries. As always, prices will vary.

Administrative and Professional Services of Funeral Director and Staff

A mortuary will charge a basic fee for their professional services. It includes a proportionate share of the taxes, licenses, utilities, and business expenses required to serve the public. This administrative charge generally includes but is not limited to consultation with the family, administrative and clerical services, preparation of the death certificate for the attending physician or coroner, consultation with the cemetery, and their twenty-four-hour availability to transfer the decedent (deceased person) to the mortuary. This professional fee is for a mortuary's basic services and overhead. The administrative and professional services fee is the only non-declinable cost a mortuary will charge families.

Transfer of Decedent to Mortuary within Local Area

When a family member dies at home, at a hospital, or an accident scene, the mortuary must pick up the body and bring it back to the mortuary. In most cases, the body is usually picked up at the hospital or the coroner. Autopsies are required by the coroner in accidental deaths to make sure there was no foul play involved. There is usually a fixed charge for travel within the local area (a fifteen- to twenty-five-mile radius). For travel outside the mortuary's service area, there is usually a per-mile charge.

Professional Embalming

Embalming is not required by law. Embalming may be necessary, however, if you select funeral arrangements such as an open casket. If you do not want embalming, you have the right to choose an arrangement that does not require you to pay for it, such as a direct cremation or direct burial. If a family wants to have a closed casket funeral service, they may opt for refrigeration in lieu of embalming.

Other Care of the Decedent

Along with embalming, there can be other fees associated with preparing a body for a viewing. Some of these include dressing and preparation of the decedent, cosmetology, post-autopsy care, sanitation, and casketing. For families with relatives who are arriving from various parts of the country for the funeral, it may be necessary for the body to be refrigerated a number of days. In this case, the mortuary may charge a refrigeration and custodial care fee. If the family needs to use one of the mortuary's preparation rooms for certain medical or religious ceremonial purposes, the mortuary may also charge a rental fee for the room.

Facilities for Viewing

Many families choose to have an open casket viewing the day or night before a funeral or cremation. The viewing is a time for individuals to meet with the grieving family and to pay their last respects to the deceased. This fee is charged for the use of the mortuary facility and staff.

Facilities for a Funeral/Memorial Ceremony

For funerals held at the mortuary (as opposed to a church), this charge is for the use of the mortuary chapel, necessary equipment and staff for the conduction of the funeral service. If you choose to have a music soloist, minister, or organist, it is a common courtesy to pay them for their time and services. In most cases, an honorarium is required.

Conduction of Services at Church and/or Graveside

Like a service held at the mortuary, this charge is for a service held away from the mortuary property. In many cases, a funeral service is held at the decedent's church; the family may also choose to have a simple graveside service. However, it is not unusual for funeral or memorial services to be held at a local community center, a private club, in a nursing home, or at the beach or other natural settings.

Other Use of Facilities

For funeral services held before or after weekday business hours, the mortuary may charge for early morning or late evening services, as well as weekend or holiday services.

Automotive Equipment within the Local Area

Funeral transportation often requires the use of the funeral coach (hearse) and driver; as an option, most mortuaries will offer a limousine or family car for transportation. Along with these costs, additional utility cars are usually required for local trips to the doctor's offices, health department, or for transportation of other participants during the funeral.

Cash Advance Items

Cash advance items are things a mortuary must pay for before, during, or after a funeral service. By having the mortuary handle a large number of these necessary expenses, a family benefits from the mortuary taking care of the numerous financial details involved in making funeral arrangements. Families can choose which cash advance items they would like to pay for and what expenses they would like the mortuary to handle.

Cash advance items usually include:

- Permit for disposition (burial permit)
- Certified copies of the death certificate (four to six for legal/business purposes)
- Sales tax on merchandise
- Motorcycle escorts
- Cemetery charges
- Clergy and soloist honorariums
- Newspaper notices (obituaries)
- Transportation charges
- Miscellaneous business expenses (Fed Ex, long-distance calls, and so on)

Merchandise

Probably the greatest amount of confusion in the funeral planning process is created when decisions need to be made about purchasing funeral merchandise. For full-service mortuaries offering a full array of merchandise options, it is wise to know exactly what you and your family want before making purchasing decisions. Here is a partial list of merchandise options that may be available to you.

Caskets

There are many different styles, makes, and prices for caskets. The two basic types of caskets are protective and nonprotective. Protective caskets are designed by the manufacturers to resist the entrance of air, water, and other outside elements. They may be constructed of varying gauges of steel, copper, or bronze. Non-protective caskets are not designed to resist the entrance of air, water, and other outside elements. They are usually scripted of hardwood or other wood products covered with fabric.

Outer Burial Containers

Also known as vaults, outside burial containers go over a casket after the casket is placed in the ground. They are designed to protect the casket and prevent ground sinkage at the cemetery. Most cemeteries require that all caskets have an outside burial container.

Urns

For those who select cremation, urns are designed to hold the remaining ashes of the deceased. Like caskets, urns come in a variety of styles and prices.

Memorial Markers

Also known as gravestones, memorial markers are generally placed at the grave in the weeks following the burial.

Besides engraving the person's name, date of birth and death, and favorite Scripture verse or saying, computer technology now allows high-resolution photographic scans to be etched into the marker.

Other Merchandise

Other merchandise decisions may include but are not limited to flowers, burial clothing, memorial folders or prayer cards, memorial register book, acknowledgment cards, crucifixes, flag cases, and shipment containers required by airlines.

Planning the Funeral: A Few Things to Consider

Funeral preparations are often dependent upon the nature of the death. Families who have experienced the gradual decline of a loved one's health not only have the opportunity to adequately prepare for the impending death, but if appropriate, they can also discuss the funeral arrangements with the dying person. It is not uncommon for someone with a terminal illness to plan their own funeral by listing who will officiate the service, what songs will be sung, who will speak, and what readings or Scripture will be read.

A recent popular and practical trend in America today is the practice of making advanced funeral arrangements. Instead of leaving the cost and difficult decision-making to grieving relatives, many middle-aged and elderly people are choosing to make their own funeral arrangements before their death. Not only is there usually a cost savings involved, but a "pre-need" funeral arrangement alleviates many of the questions about how the funeral arrangements are to be made.

For families who experience the death of a loved one through an accident or violence, making funeral arrangements is often a blur of shock and confusion. Most funerals happen two to three days after a death, and the sheer amount of decisions that need to be made can be overwhelming. For personal reasons, some families choose not to have a funeral service. However, there are many benefits to having a funeral or memorial service.

- It has often been said, "Funerals are for the living." A service provides an opportunity for friends and family to offer comfort and support to one another.
- A funeral service also provides the opportunity to remember the life of the person who died. Some of the most inspiring moments in my life have happened at funerals. Hearing moving eulogies about the quality of another person's life provides the living an opportunity to reflect upon their own lives.
- Funeral services offer what is known to be a socially acceptable place to grieve and mourn. Funerals help initiate the mourning process.
- Funeral services provide the opportunity to create meaning even in the midst of tragedy. Funerals remind us that there are a lot of things in this life that don't make sense.
- Though painful, funerals provide teachable moments for our children about the most precious gifts of life and faith.

Making funeral arrangements and planning a memorial service can provide you, your family members, and your friends an important degree of focus during the first couple days of shock and bewilderment. Your involvement in creating a meaningful service can be a useful step in the healing process as you mourn the loss of your loved one. Don't be afraid to ask for help. Though it may be difficult to figure out exactly what you want in a funeral service, don't be afraid to be specific. Feel free—yes, guilt free—to tell others "no" when the "helpful Henrys and Henriettas" are imposing their wishes and demands upon you. If you and your family get bogged down in too many details, it might be better to back up a bit by keeping the service simple.

Clarise Brady offers a few words of wisdom about the meaning she found in planning her daughter's memorial service:

"I found purpose in planning Avery's service, and wanted every element to be perfect. Because I help plan our Sunday church services on a regular basis, this was an area that I felt comfortable with—I even consider it to be one of my gifts. On the other hand, my husband didn't like this process, so he stayed away when I was planning with my pastor and his wife.

"The songs were chosen to encourage others, as we knew there would be large numbers of people there, many of whom did not share our hope. Since then, many people have commented to me on the beautiful songs and how much they meant to them. I made copies of one song in particular and gave it to many people. I think the music is so important.

"You can always ask for help in planning a service; there are people in almost every church—and even people who don't go to church—who would be willing to help if asked."

Funerals are a courageous step of faith in the difficult moments of saying good-bye. If our faith is going to be rich with depth and substance, it must be soaked with meaning and saturated with significance. Proper education and preparation for a funeral service can establish the setting for these important faith and grief experiences.

Appendix B

Grief Resources

(Author's note: I met Bill Chadwick while researching this book on the Internet. Bill was instrumental in helping me to understand how to approach people online regarding the purpose and sensitivity of Internet support groups. Despite what some people may think of Internet support groups, there is a vast movement of people receiving encouragement online in new and dynamic ways. Not only did Bill assist in reading and editing this entire manuscript, his work on the Internet is having a major and positive impact in many people's lives. What follows is Bill's story in its entirety, told in his own words.)

I was jolted awake at 2:00 A.M. when the phone rang. That gut-churning fear gnawed inside as I quickly reviewed the whereabouts of my children. We had gotten these calls before—one of the kids calling to say they would be late. But our kids were grown now. This time it was different. There had been a car crash. Michael, our twenty-one-year-old son, was involved. We sat on the sofa where we had logged so many hours before praying and waiting on nights when Michael had been late getting home. We held hands and prayed that God would give us the strength to accept whatever had happened. Headlights shone in the driveway and we rushed to the front door, hoping that it would be his truck. We saw a police car instead. I remember one of the officers saying, "I'm so sorry . . . your son didn't make it." It was just like in the movies . . . except this time it was real. My brain totally shut down. I was consumed by pain so powerful that to relive it today, even for a moment, leaves me trembling inside. It was October 23, 1993, a Saturday morning, when one life ended . . . and a new life began.

The days following Michael's death were a blur of activity that seemed to be going on without me, almost dreamlike. I wanted the world to end, to stop the pain inside, to end the nightmare. Part of me died that day with him. And the part of me that remained was dark and empty. It was months later that I awakened to the realization that my life was going to continue, and that I needed to find some means of living the rest of it . . . without Michael. That day, I understood what it means to grieve.

About a month after Michael died, I decided to sign on to America Online, just to check it out and perhaps occupy some time—something I had too much of. Shortly after I signed on, I was reviewing a list of USENET newsgroups and noticed a group called alt.support.grief (ASG). Within minutes, I was downloading articles there. I was overwhelmed as I read post after post from people who had lost loved ones. Many of them had lost children, just as I had. Some were from people in the painful, early days of grief, and others were from those farther along. The new posters wrote of a pain so intense and so overwhelming that I cried as I was reading. These people were telling my story! Almost every article had several replies posted under it. I began to read some of them and felt the love flow from the screen as these incredible people reached out to comfort each other. It was one of my first times to sign on to the Internet and already I felt like I had come home.

After lurking on ASG for a while (often several times a day) I decided I would post my first message. I was intimidated by the Internet and by computers in general. I had no computer training at all and felt totally vulnerable. I walked through my fear and posted my message. About all I could write was, "Hi, my name is Bill and my twenty-one-year-old son, Michael, was killed in a car crash on October 23, 1993. I feel like I have died inside." It took all of the courage I could muster to type those words and to click on the button that would launch them into cyberspace.

The first response I received was from a woman named Cathy who had recently lost her eleven-year-old daughter, Sarah. Her words were so warm and gentle. She wrote, "Be kind and patient with yourself, and trust that you are experiencing the grief process in exactly the way you are supposed to." This was the day that the miracle of healing began for me—a miraculous transformation. This journey that started at the gates of hell began to take me down a new path of spiritual healing. This trek in cyberspace was truly a pilgrimage out of the darkness into a new and beautiful light. I began to experience the process of surrender and acceptance. Although Michael had died and the pain was still very fresh and powerful, I finally had some hope in my life. I realize now that the greatest healing gift of ASG is the simple realization that we do not have to travel the path of grief alone.

Over the three-year period following that first post, I have corresponded by e-mail with Cathy well over 350 times and have hundreds of e-mails from all of my cyberfriends on alt.support.grief. Someone wrote early on, "The pain of losing a child never goes away completely, but it changes." I continued to write and share my anger, sorrow, guilt, and sadness with the others on the group. I would check in on the group every day and post there, emptying my heart of all the stuffed-down feelings that were deep inside me. It is difficult to explain the miracle of healing that takes place when we share our stories with each other, and I don't really know why it works. I just know that it does.

After losing my son, each day I had faced a world that seemed to be oblivious to my suffering. It was difficult for my friends to talk with me about my son. I suppose it brought them dreadfully close to their own fears about death. Some of them seemed to think that I should have been "over it" after a few months. I have heard people say, "Grief is like an open wound. It is bleeding and painful, but heals over time." I think it is different from a normal wound. I agree with Cathy, who wrote "Grief is like losing a leg. The wound of the stump begins to heal, and we learn to walk again on one leg, but the leg never grows back. There is always that place in our hearts where the leg should be." I quickly realized that the only people who could truly identify with my pain, were those who had also "lost legs." This is the powerful bond that we share on ASG. This powerful sense of community, of connectedness, slowly changed my perception, and my unbearable pain began to soften into bearable sorrow. My pain was still there, but it began to change.

Three years after Michael's death, I am still very active in the ASG community. I also opened my new home page on the World Wide Web. The address for my home page is http://www.premier.net/~zoom. The site is dedicated to Michael's memory. It includes some articles I have written about my grief journey and some great links to many other grief resource sites. One particularly interesting link is to Tom Golden's Grief Page. Tom is a professional counselor who specializes in grief counseling. His site has a place where one can post a memorial to their lost loved ones. My fear is that somehow people will forget about Michael . . . that I will somehow forget him. This memorial site is a way to keep his memory alive.

Other links listed at my site provide extensive information on such subjects as violent death, suicide, talking to children about death, sibling grief, SIDS, and miscarriage. There is a link to The Compassionate Friends, a national support group for bereaved parents and siblings. I also have a link to my cyberfriend Rebecca's FAQ (frequently asked questions) for alt.support.grief. The FAQ provides a general feel for the group and helps newcomers get started. For more information on these resources, one can simply check the

USENET newsgroup list or use appropriate keywords on a WWW search engine like InfoSeek or Alta Vista. Many messages are posted on ASG about new resource locations. It is amazing how much love and support one will encounter online! My home page has been visited over eight thousand times so far and was recently awarded the "Top 5% of the Net" award by Point Communications, an Internet multimedia company.

The Internet is bringing new meaning to the spiritual principle of community. This powerful communications tool that has begun to open up new frontiers for business, education, science, and the arts has also created great new resources for those in need of recovery and support. As we reach out across continents to love each other in our broken places, we begin to experience the miracle of healing, one person at a time. Each life is forever changed by the touch of fingers to a keyboard. Both author and reader are healed, each becoming the teacher and the student, all at once. As these souls mingle, the Internet becomes more than just another business tool or reference source. It becomes alive with limitless possibility for human love, compassion, and healing.

I have continued to participate on ASG, mostly reaching out to the newcomers there. A friend on ASG once shared the familiar quote, "To know great joy is to have known great suffering." I receive great joy from reaching out to the newcomers. Those who post may write about the anger, sadness, or guilt they are feeling, or they may remind me that "feelings are not right or wrong, they just are," or to "take it just one day at a time." The most valuable gift, however, is not the advice I get but the mysterious, divine healing that comes from simply sharing our stories. My life is transformed in so many powerful ways as I reach out to the newcomer who is crying out for that glimmer of hope that I sought only three years ago. People know me there as the unofficial greeter of "ASG newbies." My simple message of hope usually begins like this:

Welcome to the group that nobody wants to join! I am so sorry to hear about your loss. I know how much it hurts. I lost my dad in 1992, my mom in 1995, and my twenty-one-year-old son, Michael, on October 23, 1993. My life has been totally and forever changed. I don't think the pain ever goes away completely, but it does change. I want to give you the gift of hope today. You have found your way to a miraculous and mysterious place of healing power here on ASG. I want you to know that you don't have to walk through this alone. We understand your pain . . . and we care. When you are ready, we hope you will share your story with us. A miracle happens when we write about our pain and share it here with each other. Each day here will bring you one step farther down the grief path. I hope you will stick around for your miracle to happen!

My old life died with my son on that October day . . . and my miraculous new life began. If you are in need of recovery or support, I hope you will check out the resources on the Internet. If you have experienced the loss of a loved one and feel like you have nowhere to turn, I hope to see you soon on ASG. A great group of caring people are there to love you back to wholeness. I hope you will come and experience your miracle!

In this life we cannot do great things. . . . We can only do small things with great love.

Mother Teresa

National Organizations

Pen-Parents

Pen-Parents is an organization dedicated to helping bereaved families and individuals. In the United States, you can write them at: Pen-Parents, Inc., P.O. Box 8738, Reno, NV 89507-8738. In Canada, write: Pen-Parents of Canada, P.O. Box 52548, RPO Coquitlam Centre, Coquitlam, BC, V3B 7J4.

The Compassionate Friends

This nationwide self-help organization offers friendship and understanding to bereaved parents and siblings. They have over 650 chapters throughout the United States and abroad. You can contact the national office at P.O. Box 3696, Oak Brook, IL 60522-3696. Or call (708) 990-0010 for a complimentary copy of their national newsletter, "We Need Not Walk Alone," and additional information about a local chapter near you.

Candlelighters

For parents who have, or have had, children with cancer, Candlelighters is a parent support group that offers worldwide assistance. You can receive literature and local chapter information by writing: The Candlelighters, Childhood Cancer Foundation, 2025 Eye Street, N.W. Suite 1011, Washington, D.C. 20006.

National Sudden Infant Death Syndrome (NSID)

For families who have lost a child to SIDS, this nationwide support group has over eighty chapters. You can reach the NSID Foundation at (800) 221-SIDS.

Pushing the Envelope Publications

You can order Dying 101: A Short Course on Living for the Terminally Ill, 1278 Glenneyre, Suite 313, Laguna Beach, CA 92651.

Resources Online

Joey O'Connor's Home Page http://www.joeyo.com

Here you will find additional books on grief and bereavement issues as well as grief-related links to other Internet web sites. You can order books and resources online or print a fax order form. You'll also find information on Joey's other books for parents, teenagers, and children. You can even e-mail the author with comments and questions.

GriefNet

GriefNet is an Internet social service community providing information and communication on all issues related to grief, bereavement, death, dying, physical health losses, and other major losses. They offer information via World Wide Web and online discussion and support groups. You can reach them at http://www.rivendell.org or http://www.griefnet.org.uk.

Bill Chadwick's Home Page

Bill Chadwick's home page is dedicated to the memory of his son, Michael. There is extensive info on grief there and great links to other sites on grief. You can find it at http://zoom.baton-rouge.la.us. Mail to: zoom@zoom. baton- rouge.la.us.

Bereavement.org

This World Wide Web site is dedicated to grief and bereavement issues. It offers a variety of bereavement resources. Special issues facing men in grief are available at www.bereavement. org—"Men's Grief."

American Sudden Infant Death Syndrome Institute

For the families and friends who have lost an infant to SIDS, this may be a helpful site: http://www.sids.org. It is dedicated to SIDS research and education.

SIDS Network

This is a SIDS support group for the families and friends who have lost an infant to SIDS: http://q.continuum. net/~ sidsnet/.

Parents of Murdered Children

A site for the families and friends of those who have died by violence is http://metroguide.com/pomc.

SANDS (Stillbirth and Neonatal Death Support)

For the families and friends who have lost an infant to stillbirth and other neonatal deaths, this support group is based out of Australia: http://www.vicnet.net.au/vicnet/ community/sands.htm.

Grief Loss Brochure

This helpful brochure is specifically written for college students. On the Internet, access gopher://:70/00/UI/CFS/ coun/ SHB/grief/.

Live Chat Support Groups

On Wednesday and Thursday nights, you can find a live chat support group at: www.parentsplace.com. On Sunday nights, at: www.can adianparents.com.

America Online

There is a grief recovery support group that meets every Monday night at 9:00 P.M. EST. You cannot enter this group from the Internet. You must be an AOL member. The AOL keyword is Grief.

General Internet Grief Resources

alt.support.grief—A USENET newsgroup for grief.

http://zoom.baton-rouge.la.us/faq.html—"The FAQ" (frequently asked questions) for the USENET support group, alt.support.grief.

http://www2.dgsys.com/~tgolden:80/~tgolden—"Tom Golden's Grief Page," special emphasis on men's issues. Be sure to post a tribute too!

http://www.after-death.com/—"The ADC Project," After Death Communications by Bill and Judy Guggenheim, authors of *Hello from Heaven.*

http://www.trinity.edu/~mkearl/death.html—"Kearl's Guide to Sociological Thanatology," a fascinating and educational page that peers into numerous aspects of death and dying.

http://asa.ugl.lib.umich.edu/chdocs/support/emotion.html—"Emotional Support Guide," an index of support resources on the Internet.

http://falls.net:80/info/brvres.html—"Bereavement Resources," a good list of grief resorces on the Internet.

http://www.psyc.memphis.edu/faculty/neimeyer/adec/death.html—"Association for Death Education and Counseling."

http://www.cyberspy.com/~webster/death.html—Kathi Webster's fascinating and comprehensive listing of grief related links.

http://www.fortnet.org/~goshorn/—"WidowNet," a resource for widows and widowers.

http://pages.prodigy.com/caregiving—"Family Caregivers," Denise Brown's very helpful page for families also offers a monthly newsletter.

http://www.rivendell.org/—"The Rivendell Grief Page," a very large resource.

http://www.opn.com/willowgreen—"Willowgreen," Jim Miller's excellent page.

http://www.emanon.net/~kcabell/death.html—"Kay's Page," a daughter's loss of her mother (plus other good resource links).

http://iul.com/raindrop—"Raindrop," an explanation of death for kids of all ages!

http://hospice-cares.com—"Hospice Hands," great information on Hospice and other good support.

http://www.trinity.edu/~mkearl/death.html—"Death and Dying," the sociology of death and dying.

http://www.metlife.com/Lifeadvi/Brochures/Loss/loss-toc.html—"Metlife,"—a page on loss from Metlife. Good information!

http://ube.ubalt.edu/www/bereavement/—"Bereavement and Hospice Support Netline," a good source for grief support groups and hospice info.

http://www.kanservu.ca/~fairchild/grief/grief.html—"Grief and Loss Resource Centre," a good site! Great resources for children and teens and victims of violence.

http://www.denver.net/~cofgsd/Lit./LitGrief.html—"Grief: Survival and Growth," a very good summary of grief recovery. Be sure to read this one.

http://fly.HiWAAY.net/~bparris/—"A Year to Remember," Alzheimer's resources (tons) and a daughter's tribute to her mom. Great page!

http://www.traveltalk.com/cfhv/—"Concerned Families of Murder Victims," Grace Antrobus's page for a NYC group.

Bereaved Parents

http://zoom.baton-rouge.la.us/—"Zoom," special emphasis on the loss of a child.

http://www.jjt.com/~tcf/—"The Compassionate Friends: Southeast Texas Chapter" presents lots of good information on the bereaved parents real-time support group and links to other chapters.

http://home.earthlink.net/~jimncarol/ilm.htm—"Memories," a great page for parents that have lost their only child or all of their children. Information about a mail list also. Beautiful page!

http://www.inforamp.net:80/~bfo/—"Bereaved families of Ontario," a great reference for how families can help each other in grief.

http://www.gran-net.com/madd/—"Mothers Against Drunk Driving," national headquarters page.

http://pages.prodigy.com:80/NV/fgck08a/PenParents.html —"Pen-Parents, Inc.," a clearinghouse for linking up with other bereaved parents for e-mail exchange.

http://q.continuum.net/~sidsnet/—"SIDS Information Page," this is an incredible page! Great info on SIDS, a memorial gallery, and grief info. A must-see!

http://www.quiknet.com/~hannahs—"Hannah's Prayer," a special page for couples facing infertility or early child loss.

http://members.aol.com/mend7net/—"M.E.N.D.," Mommies Enduring Neonatal Death.

Memorials

http://virtual-memorials.com/—"Virtual Memorials." Post your memorial here . . . with pictures!

http://autumn.avalon.net/~goodbye/—"The Good-bye Page." Post a good-bye message.

http://pages.prodigy.com:80/NV/map/mark.html—"Maribeth Doerr's Page," a tribute to her son Mark.

http://www.mcs.net/~upchurch/jasonspg.html—"Jason's Page," a father's loss of his infant son.

http://jason.crystalball.com/jason/jasonbio.html—"A Tribute to Jason," a mother's beautiful tribute!

http://www.denver.net/~baonline/issues/PerExpFea.html— "Tears for Billy," a bereaved mother's journey of faith. Beautiful!

http://netministries.org/see/charmin/CM00227—"Lucas Scott Livingston Memorial Fund," a memorial fund for Scott by his dad, Gordon Livingston.

http://www.netzone.com/~holmes/wall/index.html—"The Fallen Wall," a memorial to victims of homicide.

http://www.execulink.com/~bapar/memorial/—"Tribute to Our Lost Loves." Brad Parameter's tribute to wife Andrea and free scans for your personal memorial on his site!

http://www.aracnet.com/~pdxkevin/memorial.html—"The Memorial Wall," a Memorial Wall in Cypress, California, for victims of drunk drivers.

http://www.geocities.com/Heartland/Plains/5516/Destiny.html—"Destiny." Lisa Barney pays tribute to her daughter Destiny.

http://www.sourcemusic.com—"Together We Can Heal." Steve Barta and "The Pike's Peak Hospice" at Source Music just released this new recording that addresses the difficult issues surrounding the loss of a loved one.

http://www.epix.net/~adrienne—"Adrienne's Garden." Lorraine Maillet has created a beautiful place in honor of her daughter.

http://www.win.bright.net/~cnelson/Memorial.html—Carrie Nelson dedicated a page for honoring her mom and other mothers who have passed away.

$\mathcal{N}$otes

1. *Helping Children Grieve: Sudden Infant Death Syndrome,* California SIDS Program, California State University, Sacramento, 1-800-369-SIDS.

2. Children need to learn that there are plenty of positive options for handling pain rather than understanding suicide as a simple alternative. The scope of this book does not cover the complex issues regarding a loss due to suicide, murder, or other acts of violence; however, there are organizations like The Compassionate Friends and other support groups that have helpful resources dedicated to these important subjects.

3. Carol Staudacher, *Beyond Grief* (Oakland, Calif.: New Harbinger Publications, 1987), 23.

4. Interview with Dr. Randi McAllister-Black, May 15, 1996, Tustin, California.

5. Ibid.

6. Karen Dockrey, *Will I Ever Feel Good Again?* (Grand Rapids: Fleming H. Revell, 1993), 17.

7. Marcia G. Scherago, "Sibling Grief: How Parents Can Help the Child Whose Brother or Sister Has Died," 1987, Medic Publishing Company: P.O. Box 89, Redmond, WA 98073-0089.

8. Charles Jordan, *Famous Hymns* (Delavan: Hallberg Publishing Corporation, 1982), 144.

9. Cendra Lynn, Ph.D., P.O. Box 3272, Ann Arbor, MI, 48103. E-mail: griefnet@griefnet.org.

10. Donald P. McNeill, Douglas A. Morrison, Henri J. M. Nouwen, *Compassion: A Reflection on the Christian Life* (New York: Doubleday, 1982), 14.

11. Debbie Gemmill, *Getting through Grief: From a Parent's Point of View* (Escondido: Beachcomber Press, 1996), 129.

12. This list was adapted from Edward Meyer's *When Parents Die* (New York: Penguin Books, 1987), 153.

13. See appendix B for more information on The Compassionate Friends.

14. "When You Wish upon a Star," reproduced from the California SIDS Peer Contact Training Program, July 1994. Elain Grier, The Compassionate Friends, Atlanta, Georgia. Used with permission.

15. C. S. Lewis, *The Last Battle* (New York: Collier Books, 1956), 183–84.